Ju 87D/G STUKA
vs
T-34

Eastern Front 1942–45

ROBERT FORSYTH

OSPREY

Bloomsbury Publishing Plc

Kemp House, Chawley Park, Cumnor Hill, Oxford OX2 9PH, UK

29 Earlsfort Terrace, Dublin 2, Ireland

1385 Broadway, 5th Floor, New York, NY 10018, USA

E-mail: info@ospreypublishing.com

www.ospreypublishing.com

OSPREY is a trademark of Osprey Publishing Ltd

First published in Great Britain in 2023

© Osprey Publishing Ltd, 2023

A catalogue record for this book is available from the British Library.

ISBN: PB: 9781472854759; eBook: 9781472854780; ePDF: 9781472854766; XML: 9781472854773

23 24 25 26 27 10 9 8 7 6 5 4 3 2 1

Edited by Tony Holmes

Cover artwork and Battlescene by Gareth Hector

Three-views, cockpit, Engaging the Enemy and armament scrap views/cutaway by Jim Laurier

Map and tactical diagram by www.bounford.com

Index by Alison Worthington

Typeset by PDQ Digital Media Solutions, UK

Printed and bound in India by Replika Press Private Ltd

Osprey Publishing supports the Woodland Trust, the UK's leading woodland conservation charity.

To find out more about our authors and books visit **www.ospreypublishing.com**. Here you will find extracts, author interviews, details of forthcoming events and the option to sign up for our newsletter.

Acknowledgements

The author would like to thank Thomas Anderson, Eddie Creek, Dr James H. Kitchens III, Mark Healy and Martin Pegg for their assistance in the preparation of this book.

Ju 87G Stuka cover art

A 37mm cannon-equipped Ju 87G-2 anti-tank aircraft, coded S7+BU, of 10.(Pz.)/SG 3 attacks T-34s in Lithuania in the autumn of 1944. 10.(Pz.)/SG 3 was formed under the command of Knight's Cross-recipient Oberleutnant Andreas Kuffner in Neisse-Stephansdorf, in Upper Silesia, in early March 1944 from 4./StG 2. Equipped with a mix of Ju 87D-3s, D-5s and G-2s, the *Staffel* was sent initially to Jakobstadt (Jēkabpils), in Latvia, but was then despatched to western Ukraine, where it was deployed against the advance of the Red Army's 3rd Ukrainian Front. 10.(Pz.)/SG 3 later operated in the Crimea and eastern Romania, before being moved north to Belorussia in June to combat the Soviets' *Bagration* summer offensive. By 25 September, the *Staffel* had been credited with the destruction of 300 tanks, while Kuffner claimed his 50th tank victory on 22 October. The unit was one of a small number of *Staffeln* that actively targeted Soviet armour as German forces pulled back through the Baltic States into East Prussia. On 7 January 1945, the *Staffel* was redesignated 3.(Pz.)/SG 9. (Artwork by Gareth Hector)

T-34 cover art

A T-34/85 serving with the 3rd Belorussian Front under General Ivan Chernyakhovsky during operations on the Vistula and Oder in the Red Army's East Prussian offensive in January 1945. The Front's tanks fought against the German 3.*Panzerarmee*. This vehicle has its tactical marking applied in white. The upper figure '64' (or possibly '61') within the diamond denotes the unit, while the lower '121' is the tank's tactical number. The tank carries jerry cans as external stores on its hull, as well as single cut-down logs stowed on either side for use as aids in gaining traction in soft mud. (Artwork by Gareth Hector)

Previous page

Armourers tighten a new barrel for a 37mm BK 3.7 (Flak 18) cannon fitted to a Ju 87G, possibly of 10.(Pz.)/StG 2, coded 'G', on an airfield on the Eastern Front in the spring or summer of 1943, while behind, another pair of armourers load high-explosive shells into the breech tray. (EN Archive)

CONTENTS

INTRODUCTION

In the wake of the German invasion of the Soviet Union on 22 June 1941, it was with both considerable alarm and irony that as early as August that year the German Army's Chief of General Staff, Generaloberst Franz Halder, confessed, 'The whole situation makes it increasingly plain that we have underestimated the Russian colossus, which consistently prepared for war with that utterly ruthless determination so characteristic of totalitarian states. This applies to organisational and economic resources . . . and, most of all, to the strictly military potential'.

Indeed, it would be only a few weeks later, as the savage grip of a Russian winter clawed at exhausted German divisions to the west of Moscow, that they encountered, for the first time, a new threat – a low, angular, fast enemy tank – the superlative T-34. As one historian has commented, it 'came as a nasty shock to the Germans'. In a further irony, however, that this 'shock' happened at all was, to a great extent, remarkable, for the T-34 had materialised only at the end of a long and difficult gestation.

Just under ten years earlier, on 7 November 1931, the Soviet leader, Josef Stalin, had stood watching down as a column of Soviet-adapted British Vickers and American Christie tanks clattered through Red Square on parade. This was a symbol of the ambition burning in the 'Five Year Plan' which promised mass production of tanks and more tanks – thousands of them. There were those within the Soviet high command, led by the then General Mikhail Tukhachevsky, who had wanted to promote a concept of 'Deep Battle' – an offensive strategy for the Red Army in which large numbers of new tanks would ram an enemy's lines and penetrate his rear area to cause havoc and defeat. As he saw it, Tukhachevsky's priority was 'the task of reconstructing the armour forces, taking into account the newest factors of technology and the possibility of mass military-technical production'.

By late 1932, however, any such strategic dreams were dogged by economic realities – a poor harvest and ensuing hunger among the population, as well as a significant decline in industrial productivity, forced Stalin to review national policies and military budgets. But he was pragmatic in the face of adversity, dismissing the lack of output in hardware. 'Concerning tanks and aircraft', he proclaimed, 'industry has not yet sufficiently rearranged itself to (our) tasks. Never mind! We shall press and support it to adapt'. And 'support and adapt' it did, for by 1936 there were no fewer than four heavy tank brigades, six tank regiments in cavalry divisions and 83 tank battalions and companies in rifle divisions.

By the time of the German invasion, combined with its masterminding of mobility, Soviet Russia had developed force mass. When the Wehrmacht invaded, it had to face an enemy whose resources were almost bottomless. The Soviet Union comprised a population of 194 million, compared to the 75 million of Germany, and it fielded an army of around five million men, plus some 24,000 tanks, 8,000 of which could be described as more modern main battle-tanks. Hitler's Operation *Barbarossa* duly became an epic clash.

Unlike German procurement policy, which saw orders for tanks being placed with several manufacturers, from 1941 the Soviets focused their output (ultimately some 60,000 examples) and subsequent design refinements on just one model of main battle-tank for much of the war and deployed it in mass. This policy worked because the T-34 was simple in design and build – in some respects even rudimentary – and thus easy to manufacture. And yet, at 28 tons, it was mechanically efficient, mobile with a maximum speed of 53 km/h, well armoured and armed with a 76.2mm gun.

By comparison, later German designs – represented by the heavier Tiger and Panther – while also undoubtedly impressive in terms of firepower and in many respects superior to their Soviet opponents, simply could not compete against the numbers of tanks which the Red Army could field. As the Chief of Staff of the German 4.*Armee* and a key planner of *Barbarossa*, General Günther Blumentritt contended that the appearance of the T-34 on the battlefield was responsible for what was known as the great 'tank scare' of the winter of 1941–42.

Many consider the T-34, of relatively simple but robust form, to be possibly the greatest and most influential tank ever built in World War II. Certainly, its wide tracks meant that its weight was evenly distributed, and this feature went a long way in allowing it to function in terrible weather and terrain conditions. To the envy of the German Panzer crews, the T-34 could usually extricate itself when it became stuck in mud and soft ground.

In answer to the threat of the T-34, Germany was able to respond with air power, and with one type of aircraft in particular – a crank-winged, single-engined dive-bomber. The Junkers Ju 87, known widely at the time and since the war by its generic sobriquet 'Stuka', an abbreviation for *Sturzkampfflugzeug* (dive-bomber), gained a reputation as an (to use an overused, but in this case quite accurate term) iconic symbol of German *Blitzkrieg*.

Purpose-built, the Ju 87 made its operational debut with the Luftwaffe's *Legion Condor* in Spain's catastrophic civil war. Despite initial scepticism amongst some senior German air commanders, it was used to devastating effect where pinpoint accuracy was required against Republican positions and ships. With tactical experience gained in Spain, from 1939 the Ju 87 went on to specialise in attacking similar targets in Poland, the West and the Balkans, its howling dive-bombing earning the aircraft a fearsome reputation amongst enemy forces. Quite literally, the Ju 87 was the airborne spearhead that offered effective battlefield support to German ground forces during their early offensive campaigns between 1939 and 1941.

Following experience gained in the air during World War I, and ensuing conclusions on tactics, the military planners of Germany's post-war *Reichswehr* began, quietly and covertly, to consider the potential advantages and practicalities of dive-bombing. Their ambitions were limited by the restrictions imposed upon them by the terms of the Treaty of Versailles, but throughout the late 1920s Germany and other nations, such as Japan, China and Sweden, experimented with dive-bombing. In his work on maritime machines, the German aircraft designer Ernst Heinkel endeavoured to incorporate precision bombing capability – an important prerequisite when striking 'small' targets, such as ships, from the air.

Junkers also carried out semi-covert dive tests in Sweden using its K 47, a strong, all-metal, high-wing monoplane fighter fitted with a 480hp Bristol Jupiter VII air-cooled radial engine fitted with basic bomb racks capable of carrying ten 50kg and four 25kg bombs, as well as an experimental sight, a direction gyro, an altimeter and a recording camera to monitor vertical bombing. Later, dive brakes and an automatic recovery system would be added in Germany.

In a visit to the USA in 1931, Ernst Udet, Germany's second highest-scoring fighter pilot of World War I who had embarked on a post-war career as a flying stuntman, international aerobatics champion and an unsuccessful aircraft builder-cum-entrepreneur, witnessed US Navy pilots publicly demonstrating their Curtiss Hawk biplanes as dive-bombers. Subsequently, Udet visited the Curtiss plant at Buffalo, New York, where he flew an F11C-2 Goshawk biplane that could carry a single 110lb bomb. Udet was excited by what he had seen.

In November 1933, following the Nazi Party's assumption of power in Germany, Udet enthused General Hermann Göring, the new Reichs Minister for Aviation, sufficiently enough for him to authorise the purchase of two Hawks, as the export version of the F11C-2 was known. These aircraft arrived at the main German aeronautical test centre at Rechlin in December 1935 and were then flown to the Tempelhof test facility in Berlin where Udet, by now a member of the Luftwaffe himself, tested them. Although the flight trials failed to impress or influence the new, incisive class of senior Luftwaffe technical men such as Erhard Milch, Albert Kesselring and Wolfram von Richthofen, Udet's efforts and personality kept a flickering flame of hope alive for the prospect of further dive-bomber development in Germany.

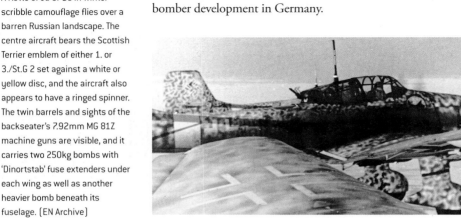

A Kette of Ju 87Ds in winter scribble camouflage flies over a barren Russian landscape. The centre aircraft bears the Scottish Terrier emblem of either 1. or 3./St.G 2 set against a white or yellow disc, and the aircraft also appears to have a ringed spinner. The twin barrels and sights of the backseater's 7.92mm MG 81Z machine guns are visible, and it carries two 250kg bombs with 'Dinortstab' fuse extenders under each wing as well as another heavier bomb beneath its fuselage. (EN Archive)

CHRONOLOGY

1894
26 June

Hermann Pohlmann, principal designer of the Ju 87 dive-bomber, is born.

1896
27 August

Karl Plauth, an associate of Pohlmann who was also instrumental in the concept and design of the Ju 87, is born in Munich.

1898
3 December

Mikhail Ilyich Koshkin, chief designer of the T-34, is born in Brynchagi, Yaroslavl Oblast.

1904
29 October

Alexander Alexandrovich Morozov, head of design development and revision for the T-34 and its engine, is born in Bezhitsa, Bryansk Oblast.

1933–34

Junkers test pilot Flugkapitän Wilhelm (Willy) Neuenhofen undertakes dive-bombing tests with the Junkers K 47.

1935
7 July

Ju 87 V1 (first prototype) completed and subject to *Reichsluftfahrtministerium*

In greatcoats and carrying rifles with bayonets fixed, Red Army troops crouch on the back of an advancing T-34/76 in the winter of 1941–42. This was a familiar sight on the battlefields of the Eastern Front. (Author's Collection)

September 17
(RLM – German Ministry of Aviation) inspection.
First flight of Ju 87 V1 Wk-Nr 4921 at Dessau, with Flugkapitän Neuenhofen at the controls.

1940

September
First series-manufactured T-34 rolls out of the Kharkovskii Paravozostroitelniy Zavod No. 183 (Kharkov).

1941

January
Three prototypes of the Ju 87D-1 completed, but awaiting Jumo 211 engines.

5 May
Council of People's Commissars of the Soviet Union issues edict that 2,800 T-34 tanks are to be built by the Kharkov and Stalingrad plants.

22 June
Nazi Germany launches Operation *Barbarossa*, the invasion of the Soviet Union.

July–November
Principal production plants for T-34 evacuated from the western Soviet Union to locations east of the Ural Mountains.

1942

January
Equipped with Ju 87D-1s, I./StG 2 holds off the Soviet push on Staraya Russa.

28 June
Operation *Blau*, the German summer offensive, commences.

3 November
Work starts on development of the Ju 87G,

based on the D-model fitted with an uprated Jumo 211J engine and the addition of 37mm Flak 18 cannon in underwing pods.

31 December
Approximately 12,500 T-34s have been built during the calendar year.

1943

31 January
Ju 87D-1 Wk-Nr 2552 is test flown for the first time fitted with two 37mm Flak 18 cannon in underwing pods.

February
Ju 87G prototypes assigned for operational testing in Russia with the *Versuchskommando für Panzerbekämpfung*.

5 July–23 August
Operation *Zitadelle* (Battle of Kursk). Total of 2,033 T-34s deployed. On one day in July, Hauptmann Hans-Ulrich Rudel of 1./StG 2 is credited with the destruction of 12 Soviet tanks, all believed to be T-34s.

30 October
Hauptmann Rudel destroys his 100th tank while flying a Ju 87G.

15 December
T-34/85 given approval for mass production.

1944

January–December
Approximately 14,640 T-34/76s manufactured in this year.

Late summer
Ju 87D/G production ends, with 771 machines built at Bremen-Lemwerder plant from a total of 1,178 ordered.

DESIGN AND DEVELOPMENT

Ju 87 – EMERGENCE OF A DIVE-BOMBER

It is fair to say that the Ju 87 underwent a metamorphic passage of development to turn it into an effective anti-tank aircraft. It was adjusted, adapted and enhanced according to tactical need. However, the aircraft existed only because of the German faith in dive-bombing. Therefore, it is appropriate that the Stuka's origins are described here.

The two men with whom the Ju 87 chiefly originated were Diplom-Ingenieur Hermann Pohlmann and Karl Plauth. A native of Munich, Plauth had become a fighter ace in World War I and later studied engineering at the Technische Hochschule in Darmstadt. He joined Junkers in March 1923 and began to focus on the concept of a dive-bomber, but his work was cut short when he was killed in a sports flying accident on 1 November 1927.

A bomber pilot in World War I, Hermann Pohlmann studied ship design before joining the Junkers Flugzeugwerke in 1923. He worked with Karl Plauth as part of the design team for the K 47 – a strong, all-metal, high-wing monoplane fighter which undertook dive-bombing trials, laying the foundation for the eventual Ju 87.

The first prototype of the Ju 87, the V1, was a somewhat ungainly, two-seat, crank-winged design. Unfortunately, on 24 January 1936, the aircraft went into an inverted spin after its tail unit had begun to oscillate while in a vertical dive and the starboard tailfin broke away. It crashed into the ground not far from the Junkers works at Dessau. It was not a good omen.

Ju 87D-3

37ft 9in.

13ft 11in.

45ft 3in.

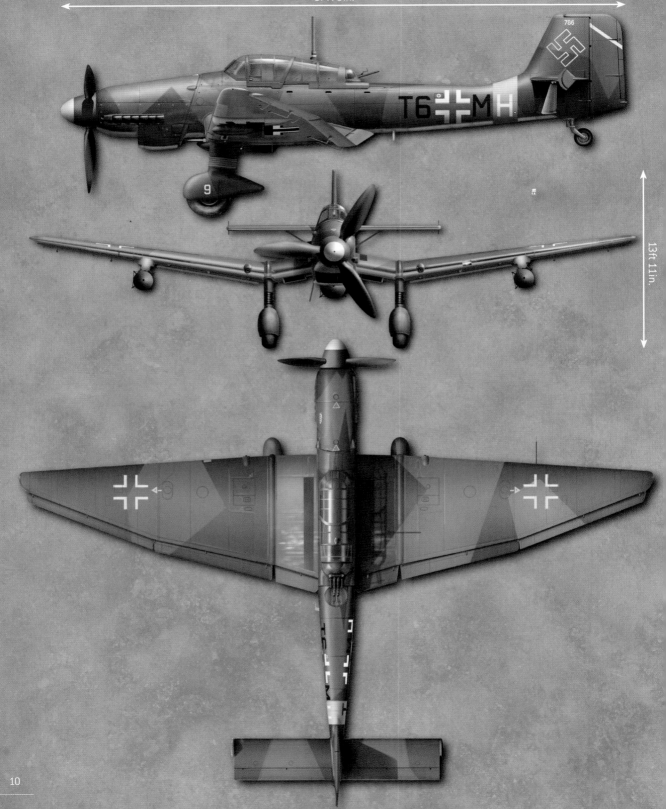

In the wake of the crash of the V1, Pohlmann, by this time the chief designer at Junkers, and his team removed the defective twin tailfins and in the following Ju 87 V2, Wk-Nr 4922, the single fin and rudder from a K 47 were adapted and fitted. This second prototype flew on 23 February 1936 fitted with dive brakes and strengthened by steel plates and reinforcing brackets. There were plans to fit this aircraft with a Daimler-Benz DB 600A engine, but they had to be dropped due to its unavailability.

The V2 was followed by the V3, Wk-Nr 4923, with an identical tail assembly, the aircraft making its inaugural flight on 27 March. Both the V2 and V3 were powered by single 700hp, 12-cylinder, liquid-cooled Jumo 210Aa engines driving a three-bladed metal propeller, and each differed from the V1 in having smaller chin radiators. The V3 also had its engine, which drove a three-bladed variable pitch propeller, mounted lower than the V2 in order to provide improved visibility from the cockpit. Further, the tailfin area was enlarged, and two faired mass balances were added for the elevators at the ends of the tailplane.

The V2 took part in assessment tests at the RLM's main test centre at Rechlin in the spring of 1936 where, on 26 May, while flown by Flugkapitän Diplom-Ingenieur Peter Hesselbach, it completed an almost vertical dive from 3,500m carrying an underslung 500kg bomb. The aircraft was built with a more conventional cruciform empennage featuring a large central fin and rudder intended to prevent spinning, while the dive brakes ensured that the V2 remained stable at speeds of around 450km/h.

Not everyone was a supporter of the Ju 87, with the aeroplane proving divisive among leading figures in the RLM. As far back as 1934, the head of the aircraft development, testing and evaluation department in the Technical Office, Major Wolfram Freiherr von Richthofen, had been unconvinced by the entire notion of dive-bombing. His reservations were founded principally on the fact that a dive-bomber would be particularly exposed to ground fire during its dive. Von Richthofen had an ally in Generalmajor Erhard Milch, the Secretary of State for Aviation, who believed that the high gravitational forces experienced during a dive would prove too great for a crew, and thus the dive-bomber was flawed. Nevertheless, the insightful Generalmajor Walther Wever, the Luftwaffe's Chief of General Staff, was an enthusiast, believing that a short-range dive-bomber capable of quick, pin-point accuracy would provide critical tactical support to ground forces where high-altitude, horizontal bombing would be much less accurate.

Ju 87 V4 Wk-Nr 4924, which made its maiden flight on 29 June 1936, became the first prototype of the A-0 pre-production series, the A-model becoming referred to as the 'Anton' series. The V4 differed from its predecessors in having an almost straight wing leading edge, as opposed to the double taper of the earlier wing. It also had a more aerodynamically shaped radiator, a longer, more streamlined canopy, smaller undercarriage fairings and a trapeze frame attached to the central underside fuselage to allow sufficient clearance of a bomb from the arc of the propellers when released. A single, forward-firing 7.92mm MG 17 machine gun was fitted in the port wing, as well as a cockpit-mounted, rearward-firing MG 15.

As with the V2, the V4 was sent to Rechlin in early November 1936, where it undertook a range of ordnance tests from early the following year. The weight of the aircraft in relation to the power of the Jumo 210 engine meant that loads had to be capped at 500kg, and only one crewman could be carried. During these trials the

OPPOSITE

Ju 87D-3 Wk-Nr 786 T6+MH was assigned to 4./StG 2 during Operation *Blau* (the German summer offensive) in 1942. The aircraft is camouflaged in a standard RLM 70/71 splinter pattern, with RLM 78 undersides, and it has a yellow Eastern Front theatre fuselage band and wingtip undersides for both aerial and ground recognition. Unusually, it appears as if the *Staffel* code 'M' has been applied forward of the aircraft identifier 'H'. The spinner tip and diagonal line tactical marking on the rudder were in the *Staffel* colour of white, as was the '9' on the wheel spat. It is possible the aircraft carried the 4.*Staffel* insignia – a knight mounted on a horse (the so-called 'Rider of Bamberg'), introduced from early 1942 – on its port-side nose.

A freshly completed Ju 87B airframe is hoisted over the factory floor at the Junkers works in Dessau. The B variant was used to equip Luftwaffe *Gruppen* as a standard dive-bomber during the fighting in Poland, the West, the Channel Campaign (the 'Kanalkampf') against England, the Balkans, Crete, North Africa and during the initial phase of Operation *Barbarossa* in 1941. Its deployment was somewhat paradoxical: whilst it earned itself a psychologically fearsome reputation among enemy ground forces and could deliver bombs with great accuracy in conditions of air superiority, it eventually proved slow and thus vulnerable when having to endure attacks by enemy fighters. (Author's Collection)

Jumo 210Aa was replaced by a Jumo 210Ca rated at 640hp. The main objective of the tests was to assess fuses and bomb dispersion patterns with standard 250kg and 500kg bombs, as well as anti-personnel bombs.

The V5 and V6 followed, both being prototypes for the B-0 series. A run of 11 A-0s was produced at Dessau commencing in June 1936 and delivered for operational evaluation to the first Stuka *Gruppe* to be formed, I./StG 162. The first A-1s were built early the following year, with 27 examples being delivered by 30 November 1937. The A-2 that followed incorporated broader propeller blades to control and limit terminal diving speed since it was foreseen that the Ju 87 would need to dive as close to the ground as possible to achieve the highest accuracy. This, in turn, meant that the aircraft had to pull out at low speed in order to reduce the forces on its airframe.

Junkers had initially intended to install the *Stukavisier* ('*Stuvi*') rudimentary bombsight into the Ju 87 following its creation in 1934 and subsequent progressive development. By March 1936, however, it was decided to fit the *Stuvi* A2 bombsight once it had gone into production, and this device would replace an interim Junkers auxiliary sight.

In August 1936, amidst conditions of great secrecy, the V4 was shipped to Spain for operational testing by VJ/88, the fighter(!) evaluation unit of the *Legion Condor*. Results were not particularly encouraging, and von Richthofen, who had been sent to Spain to evaluate aircraft in operational conditions, remained sceptical about the Ju 87. Its durability in primitive conditions was duly noted, but the single, defensive rear gun was found to be badly sited for ground-strafing and generally considered inadequate. Even its performance in its principal role gave cause for concern. Six attacks were flown with the 250kg bomb, as well as some test dives. The target line-up observation window in the pilot's floor rapidly oiled over in flight, rendering it useless for its purpose.

On a more positive note, in the dive itself, the dive brakes performed as planned, holding the aircraft's terminal velocity to 450km/h. Dives were commenced at around 3,500m, with bomb release at 1,000m. Target approach and exit speeds were, however, severely criticised as being far too slow – they were at least 100km/h lower than the minimum required to operate without fighter protection.

When it was suggested to von Richthofen that the Ju 87 be deployed against ship targets in Malaga, he scoffed in his diary, 'That won't work, since (1) a solo flight with one engine over such a wide Red territory is irresponsible, and (2) the *Stuvi* A3 sight, despite informing *Leiter* LC II at the Technical Office in Berlin, has not been sent to us. Item will be chased up'. Without the *Stuvi*, the *Legion*'s engineers believed that guaranteed hits on a pinpoint target would not be possible. Four days later, von Richthofen noted there were still problems with the V4's engine, and he remained sceptical about dropping tests with un-fused live bombs. 'In case success is negative, as is to be expected, the air attack required on a particular house in Madrid will have to be turned down'.

Later, as the three Ju 87A-1s of 5.J/88 (a part of the *Legion*'s fighter group) conducted operations in Spain, rather than undertaking close-support missions for ground forces per se, deployment was focused against precision targets such as bridges, railway yards and other choke points. It was the belief of the RLM that using the Ju 87 in the close-support role was too dangerous for the small number of aircraft that had been sent to Spain. Yet, ultimately, they were found to possess greater levels of accuracy than conventional bombers. This was an attribute very much appreciated by Nationalist commanders, and the Stukas frequently flew up to four sorties per day. Optimistic reports were sent back to the technical departments of the RLM in Berlin.

To build the Ju 87, the RLM assigned licence production to Weser-Flugzeugbau (Weserflug) GmbH at Bremen in November 1936, since Junkers would be fully committed to assembling the planned Ju 88 at Dessau. In April 1937, the RLM issued a production plan calling for an output of 35 Ju 87s per month. The first aircraft were completed by Weserflug in December 1937, and from late 1938 the firm took on full production. It also turned out six B-0s and a small run of B-1s, the latter, developed from the V9, being christened the *'Berta'*. From its various plants, Weserflug would go on to produce 577 aircraft in 1939, 769 in 1940 and 1,074 in 1941.

The Ju 87B-1 was fitted with a more powerful Jumo 211A engine, producing 1,000hp. It benefitted from fuel injection and was housed in a revised cowling with an asymmetric air intake in its upper section for the oil cooler. The radiator under the nose had vertical slats, differing from the earlier horizontal ones, and the enlarged air intake was relocated to the right side of the cowling. The horsepower gain of the new engine also meant that double the bomb-load could be carried under the fuselage centreline, and wing racks could also be fitted. The B variant had a thinner fuselage, wheel spats and an improved canopy design. The undercarriage was redesigned with aerodynamic, two-piece spats covering the length of the shock absorber. Generally, it was easier to fly since, unlike the *'Anton'*, it did not require manual propeller pitch regulation and cooling gill movement before and after a dive-attack.

The B-1/U1 was the standard variant, and it had a Revi C/12C sight that could be used for bombing and for firing the fixed MG 17 machine gun. The aircraft had a range of 550km. The B-2 was fitted with the 1,200hp Jumo 211Da, but the loading of more equipment had an adverse effect on range.

By 1 March 1939, of an RLM order for 964 Ju 87Bs, 187 had been built, and by the end of July that number had increased to 435. It was intended to replace the Jumo 211A in the Ju 87B with the more powerful Jumo 211D once 697 examples had been completed. This would mean that the earlier Ju 87As could be withdrawn from operational units and assigned to the training schools as the Luftwaffe expanded and created new Stuka units.

After the conflict in Spain, there was no sudden move to convert existing Luftwaffe units to the ground-support role. Indeed, during the invasion of Poland in 1939, the Luftwaffe fielded only one dedicated ground-support unit. Most of the Ju 87 dive-bomber *Gruppen* were viewed as being part of the conventional bomber force. Nevertheless, in the Ju 87 the Luftwaffe had an aircraft that was capable of delivering,

A Ju 87D airframe at an advance stage of construction at Berlin-Tempelhof. The Junkers Jumo 211J engine has been fitted, as has the three-bladed Junkers VS11 propeller boss. The outer wing sections are about to be joined to the inner sections, into which have been fitted the mainwheel legs, oleos and 815 x 290mm low-pressure tyres. (EN Archive)

reliably and consistently, a 500kg bomb within 100m of a target, and that was important when it came to ships, buildings and smaller targets such as trains and armoured vehicles.

T-34 – INCEPTION AND EMERGENCE

The Spanish Civil War served as the 'incubator' for both the assessment of tank warfare by the Soviet Union and also for the deployment by the Luftwaffe of the Ju 87 as a tactical, aerial weapon. Nazi Germany and Soviet Russia sent military equipment and personnel to Spain throughout the conflict there in order to support, respectively, the Nationalist and Republican causes. Ostensibly and principally, this support was meant to be seen as ideologically motivated, but behind the political posturing was the furtive hope, on both sides, of testing and evaluating their latest doctrines, equipment and weaponry in combat conditions.

At the height of the war, at a conference in August 1938 convened by the Soviet Main Military Council, a group of Russian tank men who had seen service in Spain complained in the presence of Stalin about the weak armour on the 50 BT-5 wheel-or-track cavalry tanks sent to Spain. When committed to battle, the BT-5s were easily penetrated by shells fired from German 37mm L/45 anti-tank guns – a weapon capable of blasting through 29mm armour plate at a range of 500m. The BT-5s – only four years earlier considered one of the best tanks in the Red Army – and the 281 T-26 infantry tanks which were also used there suffered from a vulnerability to fire. Furthermore, their 45mm guns lacked an effective high-explosive (HE) round.

Sagely, Stalin listened to his tank men, but he also overruled the Council's dismissal of a new design, the A-32 (the new factory designation for the fully tracked A20-G), and ordered that a prototype of it and the A-20 wheel-or-track vehicle (until March 1938, the BT-20) be built.

After Spain, future Marshal of the Soviet Union Rodion Malinovsky, who had served there, wrote that 'the trend in anti-tank artillery development during 1936–37 revealed the necessity for considerable alteration of the fundamental combat characteristics of tanks; increases in both armour protection and firepower. It became necessary to introduce "shell-proof armour" and a substantial increase in firepower'. There was a growing urgency about this since the poor performance of Soviet armour in Spain was mirrored by subsequent deployments to the Far East in 1938–39. During the battles at Lake Khasan and Khalkin Gol in Mongolia, the petrol engines of BT or Bystrokhodniy Tank (Fast Tank) models were frequently set alight by Japanese artillery fire or infantry weapons.

Soviet facilities had striven to develop 'shell-proof' armour. In 1938, the 26mm frontal armour of a BT-5-IS was slanted at an angle of 39 degrees, while the sides were slanted at 66 degrees and the rear at 55 degrees, but collectively this only provided protection against shells of up to 12.7mm in calibre. Later, another factory produced sloping armour of 35–37 degrees and of between 6–25mm on all sides of a BT-SV-2. Eventually, the Soviets did succeed in producing frontal armour 60mm in thickness at an angle of 70 degrees and turret armour of 50–60mm at 72 degrees that gave protection against the German armour-piercing 37mm shell.

Fortunately, work to overcome this problem had also been taking place since 1932 at the Kharkovskii Paravozostroitelniy Zavod No. 183 Imeni Kominterna (KhPZ – Kharkov Steam Locomotive Plant), where, in 1937, a team led by I. Trashutin had developed the BD diesel engine. Unfortunately, Trashutin's team suffered from a wave of arrests later that year, and so series production did not commence until 1938.

Meanwhile, Mikhail Ilyich Koshkin, a very capable designer from the Leningrad OKMO heavy tank design bureau, was despatched by the then People's Commissar for Heavy Industry, Sergei Ordhonikidze, to the KhPZ, where he replaced A. Firsov, the head of the group working on improved designs for the BT series. Koshkin was very qualified, holding a degree in engineering from a university in Moscow and,

Soviet infantry carrying hand grenades and with their rifles fitted with bayonets follow behind BT-7 tanks as they attack Japanese positions at Khalkin Gol in August 1939. The BT-7, which used the American-designed Christie chassis, was fast and highly mobile and, like most Russian tanks, well armed with a 45mm gun. But they were vulnerable to field gun fire and their petrol-driven engines also made them prone to fires, several at Khalkin Gol bursting into flame when petrol evaporated then ignited in the desert heat. This led to a requirement for a better armoured and better armed vehicle with a diesel engine, and Mikhail Koshkin's design, retaining the Christie chassis, became the famous T-34. (Author's Collection)

A selection of tanks built at KhPZ 183 at Kharkov prior to the Great Patriotic War. They are, from left to right, the BT-7 cavalry tank, the A-20 light tank with sloping armour, the T-34 Model 1940 and, finally, the T-34/76 Model 1941 armed with the L 34 gun. This last tank entered production in March 1941, just three months before the German invasion of the Soviet Union. (Author's Collection)

in 1934, having graduated with another in car and tractor design from the Leningrad Institute of Technology, although he went on to specialise in tank design. Held in such high esteem, Koshkin had been awarded the Order of the Red Star in 1936.

As with Trashutin, Firsov and several of his team were arrested, allowing Koshkin to return to the drawing board with a new approach for the A-20. As its Chief Designer, Koshkin was allocated 21 specialist technicians drawn from the Kharkov plant's three design bureaus, KB-190, KB-25 and KB-24, which were combined to form Section 520. Simultaneously, Koshkin oversaw the experimental and test workshops, while A. A. Morozov was appointed head of the design bureau and deputy chief designer.

Koshkin revised the original wheel or track option that enabled a crew to remove the tracks to allow the tank to run on roads. Maximum speeds for tracks and wheels were, respectively, 65km/h and 74.7km/h, and the vehicle weighed between 18.3 and 19 tonnes depending on the main armament configuration. Koshkin and his team felt that the wheel or track feature was an unnecessary element because it was rarely used and introduced cost and complexities to the American Christie suspension system. He had once opined that 'the complication of the dual-drive system for medium tanks is useless ballast, for then we have to provide the tank with more armour and better armament, and guarantee its manoeuvrability on the battlefield'. Taking along a wooden model of the A-20 for demonstration purposes, Koshkin had the confidence to voice this opinion at a meeting of the Komitet Oborony (KO – Committee of Defence within the Council of People's Commissars) on 4 May 1938, chaired by Vyacheslav Molotov, Chairman of the Council of the People's Commissars, with Stalin also present.

Acting on his own initiative, Koshkin devised an enhanced model, the A-32, based on the tracked version of the A-20, its designation reflecting the fact that the frontal armour had been increased from 20mm to 32mm. Armed with a short-barrelled 76.2mm L-10 gun, the 19-ton A-32 also featured a wide track and incorporated road wheels taken from the BT-7.

On 5 September 1939 the completed prototypes of the A-20 and A-32, worn from factory trials but fitted with new engines, were delivered to the Avto-bronetankovoye

Upravleniye (ABTU – the Automobile, Armoured Vehicle and Tank Directorate) at Kubinka, outside Moscow, for assessment. Seventeen days later, they were demonstrated before the People's Commissar for Defence, Kliment Voroshilov, and the head of the ABTU, Dmitry Pavlov, amongst others. The vehicles were able to navigate a course of obstacles successfully. Eventually, the trials led to the Main Military Council favouring the A-32.

However, upon returning to the KhPZ, the A-32, on account of its performance and high power-to-weight ratio, was fitted with weights to simulate heavier 45mm armour. Further trials indicated that the chassis and suspension could take the increase in load, and this led to the adoption of a new project designation, A-34. Koshkin had bravely rejected a proposal from the Narodniy Kommissariat Oborony (NKO – People's Commissariat of Defence) to name it after the militarily conservative Voroshilov. He argued that the designation 'T-34' was much more appropriate given that it would be a recognition of the 1934 decree expanding the nation's armoured forces – aside from the fact that it had been Voroshilov who had once commented after the purging of armour-inclined senior officers, 'Why the hell do we need tanks?' Furthermore, the year 1934 had seen the commencement of Ordhonikidze's management of the new tank production programme, and it was also the year that Koshkin had first considered such a machine.

Stalin, who saw the future role of the tank being restricted to infantry support, oversaw a decision in October 1939 to disband the Tank Corps in favour of brigades which were to be equipped with a medium tank of the new A-34 specification.

The ensuing official specification issued by the NKO of 19 December for the new tank decreed that it was to be a fully tracked tank powered by the 450hp, 12-cylinder, four-stroke V-2 diesel engine as developed by the KhPZ, and it was to feature 45mm main armour plates and improved crew vision. The tank was to carry a Zavod No. 92 Gorky-built 76.2mm F-32 main gun developed by V. G. Grabin, along with a co-axial 7.62mm machine gun. Additionally, there was to be a further such machine gun manned by the radioman, a spare carried inside the tank and another mounted for anti-aircraft use. It was to carry a crew of four – a driver, engineer, commander/gunner and loader. A few weeks earlier, on 25 November 1939, the tank had been assigned the designation 'T-34'.

The first A-34/T-34 prototype did not roll out of the KhPZ until January 1940, with the second following in February. But hardly had they been completed and were carrying out factory field tests than they were both assigned to undergo a demanding road test which would see them embark on an epic drive of almost 800km from Kharkov to Moscow, where they were to arrive by 18 March for a demonstration in the Kremlin in front of Stalin, Lavrentiy Beria (deputy head of the *Naródnyy komissariát vnútrennikh del* (NKVD – People's Commissariat for Internal Affairs), Voroshilov and Pavlov.

Things did not start well, with the diesel engine in one tank breaking down only a day after it had departed Kharkov. Although replaced, the two vehicles fell way behind the necessary schedule and failed to attain the Red Army's statutory pre-production test run of 3,000km, comprising 500km in factory tests, 300km over highways, 1,000km over standard roads and 1,200km cross-country.

Extreme demands called for extreme measures, and in this case the management of the KhPZ, possibly fearful of repercussions should the A/T-34s fail to arrive at the

T-34/76

This T-34/76 1943 Model (UTZ 183) was assigned to 4th Guards Mechanised Corps, 3rd Ukrainian Front in Romania in the summer of 1944. The tank has probably been finished in Protective Green 4BO, which served both as a primer and camouflage colour, and which offered protection from corrosion. The vehicle has a hexagonal, hard-edged turret fitted with a commander's cupola, as well as a cylindrical fuel tank, track segments and other stores attached externally. It carries the tactical number '76' in white on its turret. The road wheels are of the 'spider' type, and the middle wheel is cast steel-rimmed without a rubber tyre.

Kremlin on time, resorted to creating a 'race' between the two, still secret tanks. It fell to Koshkin and his small staff to organise things, and they did so by selecting a route via Belgorod, Kursk and Orel, but wherever possible along minor roads and at night in order to maintain secrecy.

As support during the journey, which commenced at 1600 hrs on 12 March, spare parts and provisions were loaded into a pair of Voroshilovets tracked prime movers, one of which was also fitted out for the tank crews to sleep in. And all this was to be carried out in unheated vehicles in the midst of a Russian winter with snow half a metre deep, as well as ice and bitter frost. The temperature inside the tanks remained below freezing, and as a result Koshkin developed a heavy head cold. At one point he had to return to Zavod No. 183 for a meeting and was absent for the rest of the trip.

Impressively, however, the tanks made it to Ivanovskaya Square in the Kremlin in time for the presentation on 18 March. Only the factory drivers, along with Koshkin, were permitted entry, with the space normally in the tanks reserved for the gunners occupied by NKVD officers. Koshkin, coughing regularly from his cold, explained the design to the assembled Soviet chiefs who included Stalin, Molotov and Voroshilov. The tanks raced across the paving stones at high speed, sparks striking up from beneath them.

While attaining general approval, there was some resistance and scepticism from Pavlov and the conservative artilleryman Grigory Kulik (Deputy People's Commissar of Defence), who felt the new tanks failed to offer any significant improvements over

A Russian hero – Mikhail Ilyich Koshkin, designer of the T-34. Born into a peasant family in the Uglichsky District of the Yaroslavl Oblast on 3 December 1898, his first taste of work was as an apprentice in a confectionary factory at the age of 14. Koshkin served in the Imperial Army from 1917, but later joined the Red Army and fought at Tsaritsyn. Prior to becoming involved with tank engineering, he designed cars and tractors. Following his death in a factory sanatorium near Kharkov at the age of 41 on 26 September 1940, Koshkin was posthumously awarded the State Prize in 1942 and the Order of the Red Star. The story of his life became the subject of films, and his face appeared on a number of Soviet-issue postage stamps. (Author's Collection)

An early 1943 production T-34/76 appears from the treeline, probably during trials, minus its front mudguards and machine gun mantlet. When German forces encountered the tank in numbers for the first time in late 1941, it came as a shock. (Author's Collection)

earlier designs. The fact was that Kulik distrusted tanks and was of the opinion that enemy artillery would destroy them in open terrain. But Kulik's opposition was silenced by Vyacheslav Malyshev from the People's Commissariat for Heavy Machine Building.

The testing did not stop there, and on the 24th the tanks were sent to the *Nauchno-Issledovatelniy Bronetakoviy Poligon* (NIBT – the Scientific Research Armoured Vehicle Proving Grounds) at Kubinka for further trials in which their armour was tested under fire from a captured Finnish 37mm Bofors gun and the 45mm gun from a BT-7 tank. The effects were mixed, but the conclusion was that modifications were needed before any further production could be considered. One of the tanks was also despatched to Karelia on the border with Finland for further winter performance tests.

On 31 March, after assessing the results of two months of hard trials, the decision was taken, under Protocol 848, to authorise production of the T-34. Following a meeting held between Voroshilov, Kulik, Pavlov, Koshkin and other senior figures involved with the programme, a report was issued which stated that having been completed to the requirements laid down by the Committee of Defence and having successfully completed the 'march' from Kharkov to Moscow, immediate production at the Zavod No. 183 facility in Kharkov as well as at the Stalingradskiy Traktorniy Zavod (STZ – Stalingrad Tractor Works) should commence.

However, there was a stipulation that internal space within the turret was to be increased to allow more comfortable accommodation for the commander and the loader. The increase was to be achieved without changing the angle of slope of the

turret armour, the hull or the turret ring. Furthermore, the radio was to be installed outside the turret but within the hull. Kharkov planned for an initial output of 150 T-34s. One condition was that the turret was to be increased in size in order to offer more internal space for the crew, but without affecting the sloping angle of the turret armour.

In the meantime, on 2 April 1940, the two prototype T-34s returned by road to Kharkov from their long journeys north, but not without marked effect on their engine, clutch and gearbox mechanics. The firm indications were that a T-34 could not expect to reach 3,000km without a breakdown or the need for considerable overhaul. This somewhat dispiriting situation was compounded by the fact that during the return to Kharkov, the tank in which Koshkin rode skidded and swerved into a freezing river. When he reached the factory Koshkin collapsed.

Nevertheless, on 5 June, a high-level People's Commissars and Communist Party decree on production of the T-34 stated that 500 tanks were to be built, with 400 between June and December 1940 at Zavod No. 183 and 100 from October of that year at STZ. Perhaps aware of the potentially problematic low serviceability levels, the decree also stated that Zavod No. 75 at Kharkov was to 'ensure' that 2,200 V-2 diesel engines were to be built before the end of 1940 at a rate of 210–350 per month. In reality, these were extremely ambitious targets. By November 1940, Kharkov had completed just 35 tanks and managed to expedite hulls, turrets, guns and sights for the assembly of 12 T-34s at the STZ. For 1941, ABTU would require 1,000 T-34s *each* from the Kharkov and Stalingrad plants.

Amidst all the considerable production difficulties, the first series-built T-34 rolled out from Kharkov in September 1940. That same month Mikhail Koshkin died as a result of contracting pneumonia during the return journey to his factory from Moscow in April.

By this point, the operational weight of the new T-34 stood at 26.8 tonnes, while the power-to-weight ratio was 19.1hp/tonne. The top speed was 54km/h. The tank carried a 76.2mm L-11 L/30.5 main gun.

However, the speed enforced upon the manufacturing process by the Soviet authorities resulted in some shortcomings. For example, mechanically, four gears for the V-2 engine were considered insufficient, as was the gear-changing capability which, in turn, placed stress on the clutch. The maximum speed compared to that of the A-32 (70km/h) was considered poor, as was the magazine capacity and lack of radio. Despite the request for greater internal space, the hull remained narrow as a result of the wide tracks and was thus constricted, a factor not helped by the suspension system, while the rear-mounted drive unit also required space. The 1.42m diameter turret ring could accommodate only the commander/gunner and the loader. The dual role of the former meant that at times of combat he could be placed under pressure. Furthermore, with no dedicated cupola, his range of vision was poor. There were only three exit hatches which was viewed as inadequate.

Nevertheless, despite these early concerns, by 22 June 1941, *Zavod No. 183* and the STZ had produced 1,226 T-34/76s – tanks that were superior to all other Soviet designs. But this figure and quality was nowhere near enough to withstand the onslaught that was about to be unleashed from the west.

TECHNICAL SPECIFICATIONS

Ju 87 D/G

By the end of 1940, the Ju 87 had earned for itself a reputation as an outstanding weapon of *Blitzkrieg*. During the German attack in the West in 1940, Stukas were called upon by ground units to attack specific targets in the enemy rear – troop and vehicle assemblies, fuel and ammunition stores, road nodal points and bridges – more so than rendering close air support on a battlefield. The speed of the German mechanised advance often made strikes for direct ground support purposeless.

But a hard lesson had been learned over the English Channel and southern England during the summer of 1940 when the vulnerability of the relatively slow and unescorted Ju 87 was highlighted in encounters with enemy fighters. Truly effective deployment of the Stuka could only be assured in an environment where the Luftwaffe enjoyed air superiority. This was largely the case during the campaign in the Balkans and in the opening stages of the Nazi invasion of the Soviet Union in 1941.

By late that year, however, it was recognised that the Ju 87, which in its B variant provided stalwart service, nevertheless required a significant upgrade in terms of speed and the ability to carry increased on-board weapons and specialist ordnance. Also, importantly, the aircraft needed increased armoured protection in order to operate effectively over the vast expanse of Russia in the coming months, particularly when low-level flight was required during the acquisition of smaller, mobile targets and for defence against ground fire.

Although the Ju 87D (*'Dora'*) series was conceived as a new variant intended for missions against heavily defended or fortified targets, in practice it would also serve as a response to this requirement. First appearing in the late summer of 1941, the D-1 was built around the B-2 and seen fundamentally as an uprated dive-bomber.

The *'Dora'* was 11.50m in length, 3.89m high and had a wingspan of 13.60m. It weighed 3,900kg unloaded and had a normal take-off weight of 5,842kg. The D-model was powered by a 12-cylinder, liquid-cooled, 1,400hp Jumo 211J-1 engine driving a three-bladed Junkers VS 11 propeller. This engine featured an improved, pressurised cooling system compared to the earlier Jumo 211 A and D, with the induction oil cooler being relocated below the engine unit and the coolant radiator moved to beneath the wing centre-section. The engine also boasted a covered supercharger impeller, enhanced boost and injection pump control and a strengthened crankshaft.

The immediately noticeable external changes over the B-series were a slightly longer nose resulting from the rearrangement of the coolant system, an aerodynamically improved canopy intended to reduce drag, smaller undercarriage fairings and a larger vertical tail area. The D-series was also fitted with increased armour for the previously mentioned reasons. The pilot's seat was reinforced with 4mm side armour and 8mm rear armour, while the gunner benefitted from 5mm armour fitted to the floor and 8mm armour installed over the transverse bulkhead.

Armament comprised a 7.92mm MG 17 machine gun in each wing, with 1,000 rounds per gun. The rear gunner was given extra rearward defence in the form of a 7.92mm Mauser MG 81Z (*Zwilling* – twin) double-barrelled machine gun set on a *Gleitschienenlafette* GSL-K 81 mount, with 2,000 rounds per gun which were supplied from two ammunition crates on the floor to either side of the gunner. The MG 81Z could elevate to 80 degrees from the horizontal and depress to -15 degrees, and spent shells were ejected into a leather pouch hung between the crates. The armament could be augmented by the fitment of a supplemental wing-mounted WB 81A or B *Waffenbehälter* (weapons pod), each containing three MG 81Z angled downwards at 15 degrees in the A variant or firing directly forwards and level in the B variant, with 250 rounds per gun.

This dust-coated Ju 87D of an unidentified unit bears the tactical number '3' on its wheel spat. The aircraft is seen whilst having its Jumo 211J changed in the summer of 1944, mechanics using a tripod with a block and tackle to hoist the engine away from the bulkhead. Heightened operational demands led to a corresponding increase in engine wear. [EN Archive]

As the D-1/*Trop*, the aircraft employed sand filters and survival equipment for tropical deployment. An Achilles' heel on the D-model was its weak undercarriage, so the *'Dora'* could also be fitted with an undercarriage jettison function. There was also a problem with the tailwheel, which frequently suffered from jamming or collapse

SC 250 AND SC 500 BOMBS

Configured for anti-tank operations, the Ju 87D could carry either a single SC 250 (250kg) or SC 500 (500kg) armour-piercing bomb. A single 250kg armour-piercing bomb could also be carried under each outer wing on the same rack.

when turning on poor, frontline airfields. Skis and flame-dampers could also be installed and an aerodynamic siren was fitted to each undercarriage leg.

For attack, the bomb-release mechanism could work simultaneously with an automatic dive recovery system. Offensive ordnance comprised either, as a maximum, a 1,700kg PC (*Panzersprengbombe* – armour-piercing, HE) 1800 bomb, while either two 50kg weapons or a single 250kg bomb could be loaded on racks under the outer wing. Other options included wooden AB 250 containers for the release of 2kg SC 2 or SD 2 anti-personnel bomblets over a wide area of dispersal (for which, on such missions, the wheel spats were often removed) or 300-litre drop tanks. The latter supplemented the internal fuel load of 480 litres in the main, self-sealing wing tanks, along with a further 300 litres in auxiliary tanks, meaning that the maximum fuel load, including drop tanks, was 1,385 litres. The maximum range using internal fuel only was 820km at 395km/h at 5,000m, while in a maximum load, this could increase to 1,535km at 385km/h at 5,000m – all slightly less than the B-1.

Production of the D-model commenced from the late spring of 1941, and by 6 June the Weser factory at Bremen-Lemwerder had an order for 1,037 D-1s, with peak production projected at 70 aircraft per month from January 1942, ending in December that year.

In the subsequent D-3 variant, which was also built at Lemwerder and which, in addition to dive-bombing capability, was configured for lower altitude ground-attack work as a *Schlachtflugzeug*, the sirens were removed and their housings faired over, while the fuselage undersides and coolant lines were armour-protected against ground fire.

The D-5 saw the wings of the aircraft extended by means of a new outer section added to the existing outboard wing panel, which narrowed to a rounded wingtip. This represented an increase over the wingspan of the D-3 (13.81m) of 1.16m to 14.97m, which enlarged the overall wing area to 33.68m² and lowered the wing loading. The existing wing armament was strengthened through the fitment of a single 20mm Mauser MG 151 cannon in each wing. Aerodynamic refinement was introduced through 100 per cent mass-balanced ailerons, and to assist during operational sorties, a strengthened glass window panel was incorporated for observation of the ground.

Later models included undercarriage jettison, and the joint bomb-release and automatic pull-out function was separated, with each function being controlled by its own cockpit button. Additionally, aircraft featured a sunken D/F stub aerial and a larger bomb rack.

Two night ground-attack variants, the D-7 and D-8, were produced resembling the D-3 and D-5, respectively, with each powered by the 1,500hp Jumo 211P engine.

The very real threat from an increasing Soviet armoured force that included the KV series of 'heavy' tanks with 70–90mm-thick armour compelled development of the Ju 87G ('*Gustav*') towards the end of 1942 as a dedicated anti-tank aircraft. The Ju 87G-1 was based on the D-3, but it carried two 37mm Flak 18 cannon, or *Bordkanone* 3.7, with one such weapon being fitted to the

A Ju 87D-5 of an unidentified *Gruppe* photographed in the East in the thaw of early 1945. The aircraft has had a typical winter camouflage applied and its spinner has a green or red tip in its unit colour. The barrel for the Stuka's port wing-mounted 20mm Mauser MG 151 can just be seen. (EN Archive)

A mechanic clasping a long screwdriver balances on the starboard mainwheel tyre of a Ju 87G to attend to its Jumo 211 engine. The faired housing mounted above the breech pod of the BK 3.7 contained the cannon's hydraulic oil heater and air intake. (EN Archive)

BORDKANONE 3.7 AUTOMATIC CANNON

The Ju 87G was fitted with two underwing Rheinmetall 37mm BK (*Bordkanone*) 3.7 automatic cannon (adapted Flak 18). Note the ammunition trays either side of the breech pods. Shells were not ejected but fed back on to a six-round clip and then removed after the aircraft had landed. The fairing opposite the ammunition tray contained the cannon's hydraulic oil heater and air intake.

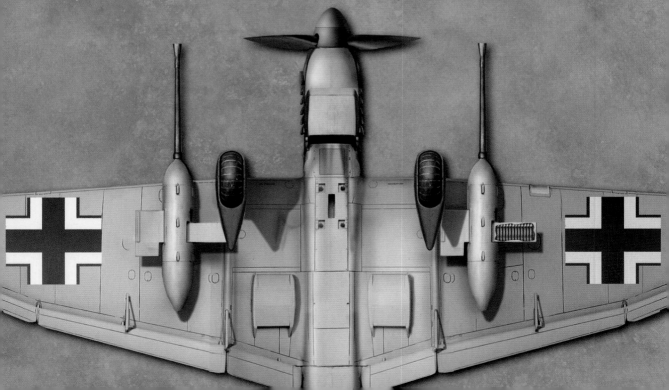

underside of each wing outboard of the undercarriage (details of the Flak 18 are included in the chapter on Combat). To compensate for the weight and any aerodynamic loss associated with these weapons, the customary under-fuselage dive-bombing release 'trapeze', dive-brakes, the additional oil tank fitted into the D-series and even oxygen equipment – not needed at lower altitudes – were removed. Some examples also had the wing-mounted MG 17s faired over, although pilots usually preferred to retain them as their tracer shells aided accuracy of aim.

The G-2 was based on the D-5 airframe and was similar to the G-1, but it had all the D-series fixed armament removed, resulting in an aerodynamically cleaner wing leading edge. Some machines were fitted out at Lemwerder with flame-dampers for night operations.

This winter-camouflaged Ju 87G of an unidentified unit has been raised for gun calibration or static firing tests at an airfield on the Eastern Front. From early 1944, the adapted BK 3.7 Flak 18 cannon finally gave the Luftwaffe a weapon which was capable of penetrating the armour of the new generation of Soviet tanks, provided piloting and targeting skills were sufficient. (EN Archive)

While undoubtedly packing a considerable anti-tank 'punch', the increased size and mass of the G-model made it slower and less manoeuvrable, with the cannon increasing drag considerably despite being housed in streamlined pods – the aircraft's maximum speed fell to 270km/h. The fully laden weight of a Ju 87G was 6,500kg compared to the 3,650kg of the RAF's Hurricane II desert ground-attack aircraft and the 6,200kg of the Soviet Il-2M3.

T-34

The T-34/76 (1940 model) was 5,920mm in length, 3,000mm wide and 2,400mm high. Ground clearance was 400mm. Models from 1943 were 6,620mm in length, 3,000mm wide and 2,520mm high. From the initial production run, the T-34 had a combat weight of 26.8 tons.

The hull, which took the form of a rigid armoured box with a rounded bow and rear, was built from rolled steel armour plates. The superstructure was sloped to create resistance against kinetic energy attacks. The bottom plate was weight-bearing and was 16mm thick at its front, thinning to 13mm towards the rear. The external rear of the tank featured a towing hook, armoured exhaust hoods, a socket for pre-heating equipment, a transmission hatch and grille.

The roof and floor plates of the T-34 were welded to the bottom plate and were of 20mm thickness. The hull sides were 40mm (increasing to 45mm in the 1942 Model). The lower sides were angled at 90 degrees, while the upper sides were at 40 degrees from the vertical. The upper and lower rear plates were set at approximately 42 degrees and 45 degrees, respectively. The frontal glacis was 45mm

T-34/76 TURRET

1. Co-axial Degtaryev DT-29 7.62mm machine gun
2. Armoured gun mantlet
3. Gunner's PT-5 periscope
4. Telescopic sight
5. Range scale elevation knob
6. F-34 76.2mm main gun
7. Commander's seat
8. Gunner's seat
9. Radio equipment
10. Power traverse motor
11. Power traverse rheostat
12. 7.62mm machine gun ammunition storage

thick and angled at 60 degrees, which effectively gave it a thickness of around 75mm, while the rear plate, which allowed access to the engine, was 40mm thick and set at 48 degrees, affording protection for the engine and transmission. Variations in aspects of design, armour thickness and welding could identify the manufacturing origin of any given tank.

The turret, consisting of several welded parts including six plates of rolled armour, the cylindrical mount for the main gun and a crew hatch, was mounted on ball bearings on top of the hull roof above the fighting compartment.

Internally, the hull was divided into four compartments. The driver and machine gunner were in the forward part of the tank, with the driver located to the left where there was a forged bulge for his head. Directly ahead of him was an episcope and a hatch, opened rearwards by means of a spring-loaded counter-balance, operating rod and bracket. Beneath the hatch opening in the glacis was a panel containing the engine oil and coolant temperature gauges, manometer, tachometer and clock. Pedals for the clutch, brake and accelerator were located on the floor to the front of the driver's position, as was a hand-operated pump for pressurising the fuel tanks.

T-34/76 HULL

1. DT-29 7.62mm machine gun
2. Main gun ammunition
3. Main gun ammunition storage canisters
4. Driver's seat
5. Steering levers
6. Foot brake
7. Clutch pedal
8. Accelerator pedal
9. Compressed air bottles
10. V-2 12-cylinder diesel engine
11. Engine air filter
12. Transmission and braking assemblies
13. Engine coolant
14. Internal fuel tanks
15. External fuel tanks
16. Radio operator's seat

To the left was the main wiring junction for the electrics, as well as an ammeter, voltmeter, engine starting button and an actuating lever fitted to a rod which connected with the linkages for the engine exhaust louvres above the transmission. To the right of the driver's position was the gear shift.

Located slightly rearwards was the machine gunner/engineer's position. His task was to operate the 7.62mm Degtaryev DT-29 machine gun which was fitted into a ball mount set into an armoured bulge to the right of the driver's hatch cover, and for which spare 47-round drum magazines were stored in racks on the right and in front of his position. Sets of four further magazines were stored to the left of both the driver and the gunner. In later models, the racks to the right were replaced by the bulky 71-TK-3 radio set, which had a range of 18km while the tank was mobile or 25km when stationary, but only four kilometres if used for two-way communication. From 1943, the 71-TK-3 was replaced by the 9-RM set, which had an expanded wave band.

The dual role for the machine gunner/engineer thus became machine gunner/radio operator. In the event of needing to evacuate the tank, the machine gunner could exit via an oval auxiliary escape hatch in the floor in front of his padded seat.

Seemingly abandoned, this T-34/76 was photographed by German troops (note the bicycle that is just visible at bottom left to which is tied a tubular German gas mask case). The image shows the bulk and sloping armoured design of the T-34 to advantage, as well as the 76mm F-34 main gun, and its mantlet, and the 7.62mm Degtaryev DT-29 machine gun in its ball mount next to the half-open driver's hatch on the hull's front armour plate, just below which are the twin towing hooks. On the side of an turret is an armoured vision port, while on top of the turret can be seen the cylindrical shape of the casing for the PT-4 periscope. (Author's Collection)

The driver's and machine gunner's positions were flanked by the springs for the Christie suspension system, and between the two of them, affixed to the lower glacis plate, was a pair of compressed air bottles used to start the engine in cold weather or if the electric starter motor failed. Above these was a TPU-3M interphone.

Behind the frontal compartment was the cramped fighting compartment accommodating the tank's commander and the gun loader, which was flanked by the suspension system for the second and third road wheels. The coil spring suspension was screened by bolted metal partitions. The seats for both of these crew members were positioned either side of the L-11 gun and attached to the turret ring, so revolving with it. In the T-34/76, the turret was built of either cast, welded or stamped 45mm plates, although there was a variation in design depending on the source factory.

Generally, the armour on Soviet tanks was heat-treated to a high level of hardness. One Soviet tank man was of the opinion that only British tanks had better armour:

If a shell had gone through the turret of a British tank, the commander and the gunner could have stayed alive because there were virtually no splinters, while in a T-34 the armour would spall a lot and the crew had few chances of survival.

To the commander's left was a vision port, pistol port and, towards the front, the turret traversing gear, operated electrically or by hand depending on whether fast or

An enthusiastic crew of a T-34 Model 1941 with a 76.2mm L-11 gun pose for the cameraman clad in typical tanker helmets and overalls. The circular port in the tank's turret hatch, into which would have been fitted an all-round vision periscope, has been plugged on this example. (Thomas Anderson)

careful movement was required. Under electric drive, the maximum traversing speed was 4.2 rpm. The PT-5, -6 or -7 panoramic periscope in front of the commander provided a wide field of view in operational conditions and was used in the targeting procedure. To the right of the periscope was the TOD-6 or -7 (Model 1941, 2.5 x 15°) telescopic sight for accurate aiming of the gun. These were later upgraded. On the other side of the main gun, the coaxial DT-29 machine gun was in front of the loader, mounted on the gun cradle.

In earlier T-34s, the main gun was a 76.2mm L-11 L/30.5 model. This had an armour-piercing velocity of 612m per second, an elevation of 25 degrees, depression of five degrees and a rate of fire of between one and two rounds per minute. From the early spring of 1941, the T-34 was fitted with the 76mm F-34 gun which had an elevation of 26 degrees 40' and depression of 5 degrees 30', and a maximum range of 11,200m.

Six 76.2mm shells for the main gun were stored in racks bolted to the turret partition, with three more similarly stored on the partition to the right of the loader. A further 68 shells were contained in boxes on the floor of the compartment, resulting in a total of 77 shells for a fully loaded tank. When the later F-34 L/41.5 gun was introduced, although the ready-round storage racks and capacity remained unchanged, as did the total ammunition count, shell storage was adjusted by using eight steel boxes, six of which contained nine shells and the remaining two, seven. The armour-piercing shells weighed between 6.3–6.51kg, while fragmentation shells were between 6.2–6.4kg.

The problem was that by 1943, the F-34 gun was effectively obsolete, for while its armour-piercing rounds were able to penetrate the side armour of the German Panther at 1,000m, they could only do so on the glacis armour at a distance of just 300m and could not impact the frontal armour of the turret at all.

Fresh air was drawn into the turret via an armoured vent and emitted through an exhaust fan in the firewall separating the crew compartment from the engine compartment.

Externally, the front of the turret was semi-cylindrical and had ports for the main gun, the coaxial machine gun and the telescopic sight. Following the removal of four bolts from a rear plate, the L-11 gun could be extracted from the turret. A further episcope could be fitted to mounts on the external sides of the turret. The roof was formed of 15mm armoured plate. Entry was through a large trapezoid, hinged hatch, and there was also a mount for a PT-1 sighting periscope, but installation of the latter ceased in the autumn of 1941.

Despite the T-34's mobility, during the early months of the German invasion, less experienced Soviet crews could be prone to driving their tanks inadvertently into soft or boggy ground. This resulted in tanks frequently being abandoned. Here, however, this T-34/76, less its machine gun, is being put through its paces on a trials range, possibly by a trainee driver receiving tuition from an instructor. (Author's Collection)

Usually, as external stores, the tank could carry a pair of shovels, snow cleats, spare track pins, a tarpaulin, two spare track links, a towing cable and shackles, and wooden wheel chocks that could also be used as jack blocks when lifting the turret from the turret ring.

A turret of improved design of cast or drop-forged build was introduced in 1942, manufactured by the Lenin Works in Mariupol and resembling a hexahedron weighing 4.32 tons.

Aft of the fighting compartment was the engine compartment, which was separated from the rest of the tank by a bulkhead/firewall in which four or five metal covers gave access to the engine and fuel system, water and oil pumps and the four accumulator batteries.

Power came from a V-2 12-cylinder, water-cooled diesel engine (*see* Design and Development) that produced 500hp at 1,800rpm at maximum power. The engine was mounted on two parallel frames held in place by 36 bolts. The V-2 was flanked by a water radiator on either side, parallel to the tank's longitudinal axis, and two oil tanks were also bolted into sponsons either side. Behind the V-2 was the transmission compartment housing the engine fan, transmission, steering clutches with brakes, electric starter, drives and two fuel tanks. The compartment was covered by a roof of two armoured plates that covered the fuel tanks, two louvre plates, a lateral tail plate and the grille.

During the early manufacturing phase, Kharkov was unable to produce a sufficient number of diesel engines, which meant that those tanks built at Gorky had to be fitted with Mikulin M-17 aero-engines intended for BT tanks with inferior clutches and transmissions.

The T-34 had a maximum speed of 55km/h, with a mean cruising road speed of 30km/h and a cross-country speed of 25km/h. It had a cruising range of 300km on the road and 227km cross-country. The tank ran on five pairs of 830mm road wheels on either side of the hull, all fitted with hard rubber tyres, as were the idlers, and joined to a Christie suspension system. The drive wheels were at the rear. The cast or drop-forged manganese steel tracks were 550mm wide and each set comprised 37 pairs of links.

THE STRATEGIC
SITUATION

It is clear that right up to the start of the war, the Luftwaffe's view of 'close support' did not necessarily include missions specifically directed at enemy armour – at least not as a priority. In its 'Guidelines for the deployment of the Air Force in direct support of the army' dated 1 August 1939, no specific mention was made about striking tanks. Rather, the emphasis was placed on attacking 'marching columns', troop concentrations, 'roads and railways leading directly to the battlefield', man-made structures and port installations.

Arguably, in 1940, despite limited action against Republican tanks in Spain, direct air-to-tank engagement over the battlefield was not foreseen as a major tactical element of inter-force cooperation. The sense was that the power of German ground forces when deployed in a *Blitzkrieg*-style assault would swiftly punch through enemy defences by striking troops, communications, fortifications, transport and rear area facilities. Yet, in just over two years, this doctrine was found to be lacking, and it was the ground troops on the Eastern Front who felt it first and foremost. The headquarters of V.*Armeekorps* reported on 15 December 1941, 'The confidence of our infantry in our own anti-tank measures has been shattered'.

This was not surprising, as the freezing soldiers of the German Heer west of Moscow found themselves having to contend with an onslaught of brand new T-34s. Indeed, as the former commander of the Luftwaffe's 2nd Air Fleet (*Luftflotte* 2), Generalfeldmarschall Albert Kesselring, wrote of the German campaign in central and northern Russia during the advance on Moscow in late 1941:

33

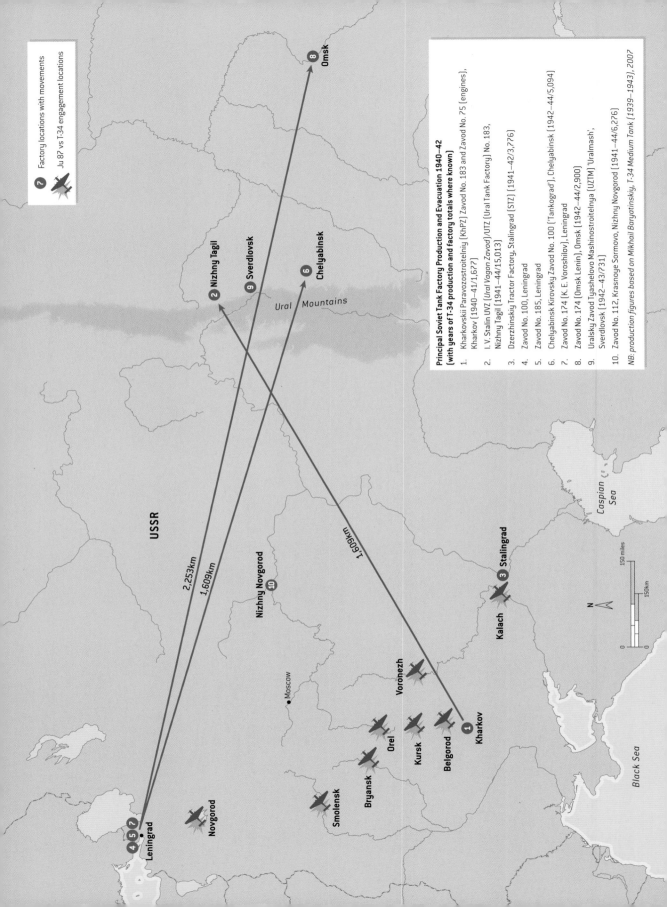

Factory locations with movements

⑦ Factory locations with movements

✈ Ju 87 vs T-34 engagement locations

Principal Soviet Tank Factory Production and Evacuation 1940–42 (with years of T-34 production and factory totals where known)

1. Kharkovskii Paravozostroitelnij (KhPZ) Zavod No. 183 and Zavod No. 75 (engines), Kharkov (1940–41/1,677)
2. I. V. Stalin UVZ (Ural Vagon Zavod)/UTZ (Ural Tank Factory) No. 183, Nizhny Tagil (1941–44/15,013)
3. Dzerzhinskiy Tractor Factory, Stalingrad (STZ) (1941–42/3,776)
4. Zavod No. 100, Leningrad
5. Zavod No. 185, Leningrad
6. Chelyabinsk Kirovsky Zavod No. 100 ('Tankograd'), Chelyabinsk (1942–44/5,094)
7. Zavod No. 174 (K. E. Voroshilov), Leningrad
8. Zavod No. 174 (Omsk Lenin), Omsk (1942–44/2,900)
9. Uralsky Zavod Tyashelovo Mashinostroitelnya (UZTM) 'Uralmash', Sverdlovsk (1942–43/731)
10. Zavod No. 112, Krasnoye Sormovo, Nizhny Novgorod (1941–44/6,276)

NB: production figures based on Mikhail Baryatinskiy, T-34 Medium Tank (1939–1943), 2007

USSR

Ural   Mountains

⑧ Omsk

② Nizhny Tagil
⑨ Sverdlovsk
⑥ Chelyabinsk

2,253km
1,609km
1,609km

Nizhny Novgorod ⑩

Moscow

Novgorod

④⑤⑦ Leningrad

Smolensk

Bryansk
Orel
Kursk
Belgorod
Voronezh
Kharkov ①

③ Stalingrad
Kalach

Caspian Sea

Black Sea

N

0   150 miles
0   150km

The T-34 tanks, which had now appeared in increasing numbers and could move even in the worst ground conditions, were a problem that imposed a terrific strain on our ground-strafer pilots, who had to fly recklessly over forests, trees and villages to deal with them. As it was, in spite of all the handicaps, we continued to attack the tanks from the air, but we could not, and did not, do them any serious damage.

An astute commander, Kesselring was more than aware of the threat and potency of the Soviet T-34. Furthermore, he was describing a reactive response and not a proactive one. Combat experience had shown that ground-strafing and light bombing attacks mounted against enemy armour by Bf 109 fighters and Hs 123 biplane close-support aircraft were nowhere near enough to make a significant impact on the increasing numbers of highly mobile T-34s. The Luftwaffe needed a dedicated tank-destroyer, but that time was some way off. For the moment, Ju 87 units would have to fill the void – but 'busting' tanks was a very different task to bombing and strafing 'soft' targets such as troops or trains, with the latter seen as the main tactical target in 1941.

When the Germans were able to deploy Stuka *Gruppen* in mass in sectors of the Eastern Front, they faced two problems. Firstly, even when attacking in numbers to effect, the fact was that by early 1943, Soviet tank factories, safely evacuated to the east so that they were beyond the reach of the Luftwaffe's conventional bombers, were able to produce enough tanks in one day to make up for the kind of losses the Luftwaffe was capable of inflicting. Such an astonishing production rate was referred to by Marshal of the Soviet Union Georgy Zhukov as 'the Russian miracle'. Secondly, operational conditions and the limited range of the Ju 87 meant that it was frequently unable to both commit to sealing off the battle area (traditionally seen as one of its primary tactical functions) as well as combatting armour on the battlefield.

And so, as the former Luftwaffe commander Generalleutnant Paul Deichmann has commented, 'it became necessary, laboriously, to destroy the tanks under exceedingly heavy fire on the field of battle'. This job was made harder by the fact that in 1941 and early 1942, the Ju 87 suffered from a lack of speed and of armour protection, making it vulnerable to ground fire and thus not well suited to the mission of low-level anti-tank operations.

However, one of the first significant displays of just how potent the Ju 87 *could* be against armour in the East came in mid-May 1942 during the fighting around Kharkov, the city which had first produced the T-34. The Ju 87B, R and D Stukas of StG 77 under Major Graf Clemens von Schönborn-Wiesentheid had been quickly transferred from their Crimean base at Sarabus-Süd to Kharkov-Rogan in the region of IV.*Fliegerkorps*. The city was under threat from a Soviet counter-offensive involving 19 tank brigades numbering around 1,000 armoured vehicles. For the next 14 days, StG 77 flew sortie after sortie against the T-34s and other Red Army types.

Early in the morning of 18 May, Gen-Maj Kirill Moskalenko, commander of the Soviet 38th Army, launched an infantry assault against German positions near Nepokrytaya supported by 71 tanks from 13th and 36th Tank Brigades. In a short time – less than 20 minutes from being called up – the skies were full of Ju 87s from StG 77 that attacked the Russian tanks at Hill 1990 near Nepokrytaya. Flying throughout the day, the unit subsequently generated a further eight missions involving 200 sorties to strike at armour in woods close to Feverowka, Krassnyji and Termouaja.

Five Ju 87Ds of StG 2 bank low over the flat Russian landscape upon returning from a mission in the summer of 1942. Nearest the camera, Wk-Nr 786 T6+MH of 4.*Staffel* has a yellow theatre fuselage band and wingtip undersides for both aerial and ground recognition. It is possible the aircraft carried the 4./StG 2 emblem on its port-side nose, depicting the 'Rider of Bamberg', introduced from early 1942. (EN Archive)

One assault in the late afternoon saw no fewer than 32 Stukas blast Soviet troops on Hill 200.9.

The following day, the *Geschwader* mounted further relentless bombing attacks primarily against T-34s clustered around Petschanoje. It was the same on the 20th when, from 0730 hrs, the Ju 87s again attacked tanks around Hill 1990 and at four more locations before evening fell. The operations of StG 77 proved an integral and important element in the German defence at Kharkov and had contributed significantly to snatching victory.

A report prepared by the staff of Marshal Semyon Timoshenko's South-Western Front for Stalin and the *Stavka* (Red Army high command) on the Front's operations between 12–30 May stated that:

> Enemy aviation played a great role in the defeat of our forces in this operation. By means of continuous strikes by a large number of aircraft, our forces were deprived of freedom of manoeuvre on the battlefield. The action of the enemy turned out to be especially harmful to our forces once encircled. Continuous enemy air attacks hindered the regrouping of forces for the attack to the east, disrupted the chain of command and threw combat formations into confusion.

This was what *was* possible given the right conditions and quantities of Ju 87s. But such victories could not conceal that fact that Stuka losses and accidents over the USSR and the Mediterranean by June 1942 were running as high as 150 aircraft per month.

The Soviets, on the other hand, had grappled with tank production problems, and Zhukov's 'Russian miracle' can perhaps be viewed with some irony. Shortly before war with Nazi Germany, several of the Soviet Union's tank factories were falling short of their production targets and struggling to improve their manufacturing processes. Zhukov confessed, 'We had failed to correctly estimate the capacity of our tank industry'. According to Zhukov, there was a requirement for 16,600 tanks 'of the latest types', but in total, 32,000 were needed to fully equip the mechanised brigades and corps.

Furthermore, it had taken a massive logistical miracle to evacuate the tank plants east of the Urals in 1941 since there was such a wide dispersal of facilities. For example, in the case of the T-34, the L-11 gun was produced at the Kirov Factory in Leningrad, while the Dynamo Factory in Moscow made electrical components. Nevertheless, ultimately, it was probably only the effect of a totalitarian regime that was able to relocate Zavod No. 183 from Kharkov to Nizhny Tagil, where it became Ural Tank Factory No. 183. Elsewhere, the Kirov plant (Zavod No. 100) and the Kharkov diesel engine plant were moved to Chelyabinsk, where they were grouped with the local Tractor Plant to become 'Tank City' ('Tankograd'), while the Voroshilov Plant (Zavod No. 174) first went to Chkalov in 1941 and then to Omsk the following year.

Crucially, this movement meant that tank production could continue without risk from the Luftwaffe. By mid-1943, the Soviet factories were bettering German tank production by nearly three-to-one, building a total of 15,812 T-34/76s by the end of the year, or around 1,300 per month. This becomes even more remarkable when it is borne in mind that the Red Army lost more than 14,000 T-34/76s in 1943 – and yet still Soviet production was able, just, to outperform such devastating losses. By early 1944, the Soviet tank forces could still muster more than 5,350 tanks and self-propelled guns.

The development of the armoured formations fielding the T-34/76s was a different matter. They had undergone metamorphic change.

In August 1939 Grigory Kulik (see Design and Development) was appointed as head of a commission charged with investigating the future of armoured forces. The entire organisation of the Soviet armoured formations was examined. The commission concluded that mechanised units should operate within a combined arms structure, but that any suggestion to disband the tank corps, as had come from Dmitry Pavlov, should be rejected. Tanks should be deployed to support infantry and cavalry breakthroughs, although in cases where an enemy was in retreat, they could operate independently.

Thus, the proposal was to create infantry support tank brigades and independent brigades. When this revised force structure was placed before the Main Military Council, it opined that experience in Poland 'demonstrated the difficulty of command and control during operations of tank corps, as well as their cumbersome size', and that 'separate tank brigades operated better and were more mobile'. There was no requirement for a corps formation, and on 7 December 1939, the Defence Ministry ordered the disbandment of the existing tank corps. It would be replaced by motorised rifle divisions that might be augmented with armour to become mechanised divisions, and on 21 November it was decided to create up to 15 motorised divisions by the first half of 1941, each with 275 tanks.

However, the poor performance of Soviet mechanised formations during the Russo-Finnish War, followed by the speed of the German advance through the West

Workers sit proudly on the fruits of their labours as another newly completed T-34/76 leaves the assembly line at Zavod No. 112 in Krasnoye Sormovo. Note the face of the worker peering through the hatch from the driver's position. In the background, another tank is hoisted down to the line. Between 1941–44, Zavod No. 112 built 6,276 T-34s. (Getty Images)

in the spring of 1940, forced a profound rethink. The *Stavka* acidly accepted that the strategy deployed by German forces during the attack on Poland and the West had been influenced and shaped to some extent by the very doctrine which had been abandoned by the Red Army some years before.

The U-turn came. On 6 July 1940, the NKO was ordered to establish no fewer than nine new mechanised corps, with 20 more following by March 1941. Each corps was to comprise, on paper at least, two tank divisions with a total of 126 heavy KV tanks and 420 T-34 medium tanks, plus one mechanised division made up of 275 light tanks and 49 armoured cars. This would have seen the creation of an armoured force numbering more than 12,000 T-34s – but it never happened, despite optimistic projections being presented to Stalin. The NKO forecast that it would take until at least 1943 for industrial output to reach anywhere near the requirement for 29 mechanised corps.

Nevertheless, even as tensions escalated between Soviet Russia and Nazi Germany in early 1941, the military-bureaucratic machine endeavoured to progress with the plan. By June, 29 corps had been 'formed', although by the following month only nine existed in any form of strength or readiness to one degree or another. These nine basically weak corps, lacking sufficient training and positioned close to the western border of the Soviet Union, could field just 1,475 T-34s with which to repel the field-grey onslaught which was to come. However, this was the kernel of something that would grow significantly through tenacity, guile and engineering to ultimately defeat the armies of the Third Reich.

THE COMBATANTS

Ju 87 CREW TRAINING

Following its official formation in 1935, the Luftwaffe established an infrastructure of *Flugzeugführerschulen* at which young men with gliding experience who were considered sufficiently proficient could undertake elementary training in powered aircraft with a view to flying on military service. Aspiring trainee pilots would qualify through a series of A, B and C certificates depending on a scale of aircraft weight classifications. Once qualified, a pilot, or observer, navigator, radio operator or air gunner, would be assigned to a more advanced training school specialising in a given branch of aviation.

In mid-1936, personnel and equipment from I./StG 165, which had been formed at Kitzingen the previous year, were used to form an initial cadre – designated the *Sturzkampflehrgang Kitzingen* – to practise and develop dive-bomber and ground-attack tactics. A second cadre, known as the *Sturzkampflehrgang Barth*, was formed at Barth from IV.(Stuka)/LG 1 with support from Kitzingen-based instructors.

The most renowned Stuka pilot of all, Hans-Ulrich Rudel, recalls how, in 1938, while undergoing his flight training, his cadre made a visit to an anti-aircraft gunnery school on the Baltic coast. Their presence coincided with an unexpected visit by Generalfeldmarschall Hermann Göring. At the end of a speech to the assembled trainees, Göring asked for volunteers to become officers for the newly-formed Stuka units. It was this episode that set Rudel off on his course to military distinction.

However, as the Luftwaffe was in the process of building up, cooperation with the army and the notion of army and battlefield support was something that was largely neglected. Nevertheless, Luftwaffe air units and specialist reconnaissance and army support officers did occasionally participate in manoeuvres and other exercises conducted by the Heer, and this served to offer some practical benefit to those from both services who were involved with training and instruction. Inherently, these joint manoeuvres also helped to generate understanding, thus promoting deeper levels of inter-service cooperation.

Encouragingly, in 1937, large-scale joint Heer–Luftwaffe manoeuvres took place, in which amongst other things the Luftwaffe was used to carry out exercise missions in order to give troops an opportunity to practice active and passive air defence measures. Despite this, senior Luftwaffe commanders remained of the opinion that air support for the army should continue to be indirect through action against the enemy rear, rather than effecting direct support on the battlefield. So it was that, despite the albeit limited experience of direct battlefield support gained in the Spanish Civil War, as late as 1939, operations by the Stuka units were to focus on rear area targets.

Meanwhile, based at Insterburg, in East Prussia, was I./StG 160, which had been formed in the summer of 1938 with Hs 123 biplane ground-attack aircraft. By November, however, the *Gruppe* had not been assigned a *Kommandeur*, and so the *Kapitän* of 1.*Staffel*, Leutnant Werner Hozzel, was appointed to take over interim command at the time the *Gruppe* was due to convert to the Ju 87B, relocating from Silesia to Insterburg. After having transferred and then having handed over their Henschels, the crews of I./StG 160 collected their new aircraft from a local air depot. Hozzel recalled his unit's early experiences with the Ju 87:

> We first concerned ourselves with the details of instrumentation and with the hydraulic system, especially developed for dive-bombing, and finally with the bomb release. After a few short briefing flights, the crews felt at ease in their closed cabins. We still had to learn how to control the Ju 87 in nose-diving. There existed no Stuka school at that time, but there was the airfield at Barth, in Pomerania, where a Stuka training *Gruppe* was being built up. The instructors there first had to get familiar, by making test flights, with the new machine before they could pass their experience and skill on to the other Stuka *Gruppen*. We therefore helped ourselves as best we could.
>
> We first singled out the crews. The pilot and his backseater – the latter also acting as gunner – had to be a real team; one that had to depend on each other, for better and worse. If, after a while, it was found that the pair did not harmonise, the men were replaced until pilots and their backseaters had found themselves.

Rudel, as an oberfähnrich, was assigned to I./StG 168 at Graz-Thalerhof in Austria:

> 1 June, 1938, I arrive at Graz, in the picturesque province of Steiermark, to report to a Stuka formation as officer senior cadet. It is three months since German troops marched into Austria and the population is enthusiastic. The squadron, which is stationed outside the town in the village of Thalerhof, has recently received the Ju 87 type; the single-seater Henschel will no longer be used as a dive-bomber. Learning to dive at all angles up to 90 degrees, formation flying, aerial gunnery and bombing are the fundamentals of the new arm. We are soon familiar with it. It cannot be said that I am a rapid learner.

Meanwhile, in April 1939, the Kitzingen and Barth *Lehrgang* were combined to form a single Dive-Bomber Flying School, the *Sturzkampffliegerschule Kitzingen*. This title was retained until 1 November 1939 when the school moved to Insterburg and was renamed as the *Sturzkampffliegerschule Insterburg*. The Staff of a second such school was formed in Otrokowitz in December and designated the *Sturzkampffliegerschule Otrokowitz*, but on 16 January 1940 it was renamed *Sturzkampffliegerschule 2*, with the Insterburg-based unit becoming *Sturzkampffliegerschule 1*.

At Insterburg, the men of I./StG 160 carried out flight and dive-bombing training over the surrounding forests of East Prussia. Nose-diving flights aimed towards a marked circle, ten metres in diameter, were monitored from a nearby observation tower that had been especially erected for the job. Hozzel recalled:

We approached our target at an altitude of 5,000m, extended the dive brakes shortly before the target, then brought the target into the lower cockpit window below our feet. When it disappeared at the rear edge, we put the aircraft down at a dive angle of 70 degrees. With the fuel shut off, the aircraft quickly gained speed by its own weight, whilst the dive brakes kept it at a steady pace of 450km/h.

We aimed through a reflector sight, keeping the whole aircraft in the centre of the target and allowing for velocity and direction of the wind, with the aid of the right lead angles. A continuously adjustable red marking arrow was mounted on the altimeter, set to local altitude above mean sea level, from which the required bomb releasing altitude could be set. When passing that altitude in a dive, a loud and clear horn signal was sounded, warning the pilot to press the bomb-release button on the control stick and pull out the aircraft. By pressing the releasing button, we also automatically actuated the hydraulic recovery device which aided the pilot under the heavy G-load encountered in steep dive recoveries.

The normal bomb-releasing altitude was close to 700m. Experienced pilots would also venture down to 500m in order to increase bombing accuracy. This, however, was the minimum pull-out radius needed to clear the ground in time. Below that, there was no hope left.

Once crews had mastered the art of nose-diving in the Ju 87, they next undertook bomb 'throwing' while diving, firstly using cement practise bombs and then, when considered sufficiently proficient, with live ordnance. Bombs had to be dropped within the ten-metre circle to be viewed as a 'hit'.

Oberleutnant Helmut Mahlke was posted to the *Sturzkampffliegerschule Kitzingen* on 1 July 1939, having previously served as a maritime observer/navigator flying He 60s with 1./Bordfl.Gr. 196. He viewed his new posting as a significantly positive career development. 'I was like the cat that had swallowed the cream, happy beyond words at the prospect of getting back into the pilot's seat and holding the stick in my own hands again'. Nevertheless, Mahlke found that attaining a level of competence in dive-bombing was difficult, as he explains in his memoirs:

The most important part of our training was, of course, precision dive-bombing practice. To ensure the necessary accuracy, the Stuka had to dive at an angle of at least 70–80

Oberstleutnant Paul-Werner Hozzel photographed after receiving the Oakleaves to the Knight's Cross on 14 April 1943. He was among the very first Stuka pilots to receive the Knight's Cross for his actions in Norway in early 1940. After leading I./St.G 1 in the Mediterranean, where his *Gruppe* saw intensive operations against Allied shipping, he was appointed *Kommodore* of StG 2 on 16 October 1941. From then, through to 28 February 1943, he took part in, and oversaw, many attacks against Soviet armour. He is believed to have flown some 400 missions in total. (EN Archive)

1. Fuel pressure gauge	14. Engine priming pump	26. Cockpit ventilation control	39. Cockpit lights
2. Radio panel	15. Oil cooling flap control	27. Automatic starter	40. Circuit breaker panel
3. Magnetic compass	16. Supercharger pressure gauge	28. Canopy latch handle	41. Seat adjustment handle
4. Cockpit light controls	17. Rev counter dial	29. Main electrics panel	42. Throttle
5. Starter switch	18. Airspeed indicator	30. Fuel contents gauge	43. Propeller pitch control lever
6. Rate of climb indicator	19. Clock	31. Bomb selection switch	44. Magnetos
7. Altimeter	20. Revi C/12C sight	32. Radio electrics panel	45. War emergency power control
8. Bomb window control	21. Loading buttons	33. Bomb arming handle	46. Switch and test box
9. Coolant temperature gauge	22. Test lamp	34. Engine priming pump	47. Water-cooler flaps indicators
10. Compass repeater	23. Fuel contents gauges	35. Rear-view mirror	48. Rudder pedals
11. Turn-and-bank indicator	24. Fuel-metering hand primer pump	36. Oil temperature gauge (1)	49. Pilot's seat and cushion
12. Bomb altimeter	25. Instrument shroud padding	37. Oil temperature gauge (2)	
13. KG 12A control column		38. Main electrics switch	

degrees. At first, an angle of 70 degrees seemed to me to be impossibly steep, but it soon became routine. What I found much more difficult was estimating the correct height at which to release the bomb. The altimeter couldn't unwind fast enough when the Stuka was in a near-vertical dive and always lagged a little behind the machine's actual height. The pilot, therefore, had to rely mainly on his own judgement as to his altitude – or lack thereof!

'Diving with and without bombs was part of our daily routine', Hozzel remembered. 'Besides that, we also began training in *Staffeln* as combat flying practice with the whole *Gruppe*'.

Mahlke also paid tribute to the role of the 'backseat' rear gunners:

The demands made upon the gunner sitting in the rear of the cockpit of the Stuka were far greater than those required of the pilot. Facing rearwards, monitoring the airspace behind the machine and ready to let fly at any attacking fighter approaching from astern, he would often be forced to his knees by some of the pilot's more violent defensive manoeuvres. Yet I never once heard a single word of complaint from any of our gunners. They did their job with commendable courage and resilience.

The training emulated that given to Luftwaffe fighter pilots, which assisted in increasing the pilots' skills of manoeuvrability. According to Hozzel:

They had to become part of the aircraft. This included starts and landings on short, bumpy emergency airfields. Occasional crash-landings could not be avoided, but this preliminary training proved most useful in anticipation of risky landings in unknown regions in the following war.

Once this aspect of training was completed, crews were give tactical instruction for envisaged operational situations, including navigation, weather briefings, understanding of the ground and air environments, anti-aircraft fire, ammunition and its replenishment, fuse-setting, take-off formations, unit leader recognition and codes, formation flying, operational altitudes, attack signals, return formations and altitudes and landing orders and procedures.

The three *Staffelkapitänen* of I./StG 160 were rotated to the *Sturzkampflehrgang Barth* in order to exchange experiences with the senior officers there, and to engage in practice with them. Instruction at Barth, which was overseen for a period by Oberstleutnant Günter Schwarzkopff, a former World War I pilot who would command IV.(Stuka)/LG 1 and StG 165. Training took the form of lectures, as well as small- and large-scale tactical formation flying. A memorial to Schwarzkopff records that, 'Diving skill and accuracy were of paramount importance, and under his personal leadership were continually improved and bettered. Releasing bombs when diving was scientifically and practically examined and lessons were painstakingly learned from their dedicated experiments'.

Thus, by the time Germany invaded Poland in September 1939, the crews of its Stuka squadrons had reached a level of exceptional proficiency. Yet when they went into battle they soon discovered that although dive-bombing would form a

ALWIN BOERST

Alwin Boerst was born on 20 October 1910 in Osterode, a town on the southwestern edge of the Harz mountains, the youngest of nine sons of a conservator. At school, the young Alwin developed a keen interest in gliding and built his own craft. In the summer of 1933 he flew from the Wasserkuppe and gained his A- and B licenses. At technical university in Göttingen Boerst studied mathematics, physics and aeronautical science, and he also took part in gliding competitions from the Wasserkuppe.

In April 1934, Boerst joined the Wehrmacht and was posted to a transport battalion, but by 1937 he had switched to the Luftwaffe and was serving as an unteroffizier in the bomber unit 7./KG 157 *Boelcke* equipped with He 111s at Delmenhorst. The following year he underwent further flight training and was transferred as an oberfähnrich to 3./StG 163. Boerst was promoted to leutnant on 1 September 1938. The following May his *Staffel* was redesignated 3./StG 2, and Boerst would remain with his unit's parent *Gruppe* for the remainder of his war.

In July 1939 he paired up with his rear-gunner Ernst Filius, and the two men would serve together in all the campaigns in which StG 2 fought. Boerst flew 39 missions in Poland and became the most successful pilot in I./StG 2, being awarded the Iron Cross Second Class on 27 September 1939. In the campaign against France in May 1940, he led the first dive-bombing attack against Fort

Eben Emael and then the bridges at Aalst, in Belgium. One day, whilst based in France, Boerst came across an abandoned and emaciated Cocker Spaniel which he took into his care and nursed back to health. It remained at his side for some time. By the end of operations over France, Boerst had flown 113 operational missions and had been awarded the Iron Cross First Class. During the campaign against England in August 1940 he was promoted to oberleutnant.

Boerst went on to undertake operations over the Balkans and Greece, where he flew 22 missions, including attacks on ships at Piraeus. Over Crete he was credited with the sinking of a British destroyer, and inflicted damage to another.

Shortly before Barbarossa, he was appointed *Staffelkapitän* of 3./StG 2. On 2 September 1941, Boerst chalked up his 300th mission when he bombed a bridge over the Newa near Tyrkowo. He was awarded the Knight's Cross on 5 October 1941 in recognition of this mission milestone.

As a Ju 87 pilot, Boerst became adept at destroying Soviet tanks, and accounted for six of them in his first month of operations in Russia. He subsequently flew missions over many 'hotspots' including Demyansk, Kholm, Voronezh, Rostov, the Don bend and Stalingrad. Then, on 28 August 1942, having flown 600 missions, he was sent back to the Reich for a period of rest. On 28 November, after 624 missions, and with the rank of hauptmann, he was awarded the Oakleaves to the Knight's Cross.

Boerst accounted for more enemy tanks at the battle of Kursk, and was appointed *Kommandeur* of I./StG 2 on 24 September 1943.

He flew the 37mm cannon-armed Ju 87G-1 for the first and last time on 30 April 1944 on a mission from which neither he nor Oberfeldwebel Filius returned. The dramatic circumstances of their demise are detailed in the Combat chapter. Alwin Boerst was promoted to major and awarded the Swords to the Knight's Cross posthumously on 6 April 1944. He is known to have flown between 1,050 and 1,060 combat missions.

Hauptmann Alwin Boerst (left) and his gunner, Oberfeldwebel Ernst Filius, in their Ju 87D that has been marked with the Scottish Terrier marking of 3./StG 2. (EN Archive)

prerequisite task, they would also be called upon regularly to carry out *ground-attack* sorties. For example, one unit operating over Poland, 3.(St)/186(T), formed to fly the intended carrier-borne Stuka, aside from dive-bombing carried out regular close-support and ground-attack missions, including strafing enemy troops, command posts and machine gun nests, knocking out Flak batteries and attacking armoured trains and freight yards.

Such missions became commonplace during subsequent operations over Belgium and France in May 1940, and in the Balkans the following year. And yet it would not be until 2 May 1941 – less than two months before the commencement of Operation *Barbarossa* – that the Operations Staff of the Commander-in-Chief of the Luftwaffe issued a 'Tactics Bulletin for the Conduct of Operations by Close Support Air Units'.

T-34 CREW TRAINING

Much of the initial impetus and direction in the training of crews for the T-34 – and other Soviet tank types – at the time war broke out between Nazi Germany and the Soviet Union was initiated by a handful of vigorous and intelligent field commanders. Men like Semyon Ilyich Bogdanov, who was one of the first Red Army tank commanders to engage German forces at the opening of *Barbarossa*.

Born in Saint Petersburg on 10 September 1894 into a worker's family in the Pskov Governorate, Bogdanov commenced his own working life at the age of 12 as an apprentice metal-worker in Russia's largest military-industrial complex, the Putilov Works, in what was then Saint Petersburg. He later served in the Tsar's Russian Army and as an infantryman, rising to become an officer, but then joined the Red Army in 1918 during the civil war. By January 1937 Bogdanov was commanding the 9th Mechanised Brigade in the Leningrad military district, although he subsequently fell victim to Stalin's Purges – one of approximately 35,000 officers to suffer.

Having survived the ordeal of a labour camp in Siberia, Bogdanov was one of those called back when the Red Army needed experienced military leadership in the wake of its poor performance in Poland and Finland. In the months leading up to what became known as the Great Patriotic War, and as part of the Red Army's 1940 review of armoured strategy and a significant increase in its armoured strength (*see* The Strategic Situation), Bogdanov was appointed commander of 30th Tank Division in 4th Army's 14th Mechanised Corps, equipped with T-26 and T-38 tanks.

Although 4th Army had held detailed briefings in the spring of 1941 with its divisional commanders and other senior officers on the eventuality of a national military emergency, when German forces invaded on 22 June, the Red Army's mechanised corps was still in the process of reorganisation in the frontier districts. This meant that it was woefully prepared for what would follow.

Twenty-four hours prior to the commencement of *Barbarossa*, Bogdanov had his division carrying out field training exercises to the southwest of Pruzhany, where his food supplies were also stored. The reality was that most of his tankers were new recruits, and the few that had experience were in command positions. This meant that

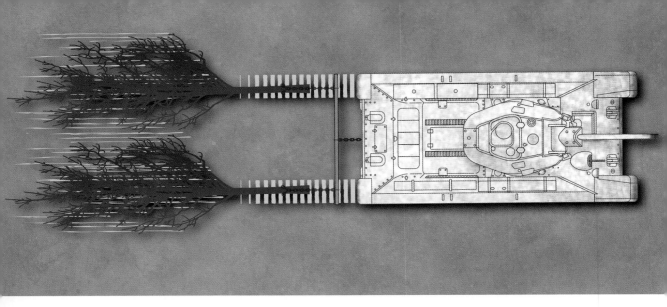

As a makeshift tactic to conceal the location and movement of tanks in snow from the air, T-34 crews would rig up a cut-down log and attach it to the hull's rear lower armour plate. A pair of cut-down fir trees would then be tied to the log to act as 'brushes' to cover the tank's tracks as it moved forward.

tank commanders were appointed as platoon commanders, and drivers and mechanics were propelled to become assistant company commanders. All in all, it was very apparent that the tank units were manned by personnel who had little idea of the principles of sophisticated armoured warfare. Bogdanov knew this, but there was nothing he could do about it.

The Chief of Staff of 4th Army, General Leonid Sandalov, happened to make a visit to the division at the time, and he was dismayed at what he observed. Shocked at how ill-prepared the tank crews seemed to be, he later wrote that they 'operated with no coordination', and that 'tanks became confused on the course and often stopped to determine their location'. Bogdanov complained to Sandalov that his light tanks equipped with 38mm and 45mm guns were old models and worn out, while the Army's supply depots were lacking in parts or held rusting, out-of-commission tanks. As he commented to Sandalov, 'If a bottle of wine is diluted with three bottles of water, this will also not be wine'.

Once war started, Bogdanov proved an insightful armoured commander who placed great emphasis on the importance of training. He would command armoured formations during the battle of Moscow, culminating in leadership of 12th Tank Corps based in the Moscow Military District. He went on to become commander of 6th Mechanised Corps during operations around Kotelnikovo in December 1942, after which he led 9th Tank Corps at Kursk. From September 1943 Bogdanov was commander of 2nd Tank Army (from 20 November 1944, 2nd Guards 'Red Banner' Tank Army). He was made a Hero of the Soviet Union on 11 March 1944 and again on 4 June 1945 for his leadership of 2nd Guards Tank Army during the offensives against the Vistula and Oder rivers. Three days earlier, he had been promoted to Marshal of Tank Forces.

The Red Army's foremost senior tank commander was Pavel Semyonovich Rybalko, who was born in Ukraine on 4 November 1894. His father worked in a sugar refinery, and like Bogdanov and countless others, Rybalko started his working life young – at the age of 13. He served in the Tsar's army from 1914 and was decorated for bravery. He left the front in October 1917 to join the Bolshevik fighting force, the Red Guard, and led revolutionary partisans against German forces and Ukrainian nationalists. Subsequently, after joining the Communist Party, he became a commissar and also received the Order of the Red Banner for his conduct in the Russian Civil War, during which he was wounded no fewer than 14 times.

Rybalko's focus then shifted from political to military matters. After training as a cavalryman, he served as aide in the Motor-Mechanised Directorate and became an advocate of the maligned mechanised 'Deep Battle' (*see* Introduction) strategy. In 1926 Rybalko gained a place at the Red Army Military Academy, where he studied for a staff appointment. In 1931 he was a student at the Frunze Military Academy, and later spent a year in China as an advisor to cavalry units fighting the Japanese in Manchuria. In 1937 Rybalko was appointed the Soviet military attaché to Poland, but he returned to the USSR in September 1939 following the German invasion of that country. In 1940 Rybalko was one of those officers who enjoyed rapid promotion in the wake of the Purges, being elevated to the rank of major general.

When the Germans invaded on 22 June 1941, Rybalko was serving as an instructor at the Kazan Armoured School. The latter offered courses based on principles learned during the time of inter-war Soviet-Nazi cooperation. These included advanced instruction for assistant commanders of tank companies, technical officers at battalion and brigade-levels, as well as fuel specialists. In his position, Rybalko was able to gain a deep understanding of both tank warfare and developments in mechanics and technology. But he became bored, and with the Motherland under assault, he craved for an operational assignment. In this he was successful, being assigned as the deputy commander for infantry with 3rd Tank Army in May 1942.

Rybalko, however, quickly recognised that he was not well-versed in the operation of the Red Army's latest tanks, including the T-34. Pulling on a clean set of overalls, he presented himself at the tank park of one of the component brigades of 3rd Tank Army. Here, he underwent instruction on handling the T-34, its mechanics, components and instruments. He watched the tank in operation. He spoke with drivers and mechanics and spent 15 hours inside one as it sped across various types of terrain. His goal was to learn everything there was to know about the T-34.

In July 1942 Rybalko was appointed to lead 5th Tank Army, and he subsequently went on to have an illustrious career. As commander of 3rd Guards Tank Army, he was involved in the Battle of Berlin in the spring of 1945. After the war Rybalko was appointed commander of the mechanised forces of the Red Army, and he is recognised as being one of the best Soviet specialists in armoured warfare.

Commanders like Bogdanov and Rybalko understood how vital good training was to success on the battlefield, and they pressed its importance to the Soviet leadership. New tank training regiments were established at Chelyabinsk, Nizhniy Tagil and Sverdlovsk, while schools were set up at Kurgan, Ufa, Ulyanovsk and Satarov. Novice crews would spend eight weeks undergoing basic training before being assigned to a training regiment close to a tank factory. While the regiments could output around 2,000 new crews per month, many were needed by the factories, which suffered from a continual shortage of workers. Crews that did get assigned a tank would then be sent via rail to the front.

As the war progressed, at a junior level, tank training became more hurried and less organised. One young cadet who went through the training 'system' in 1941–42, such as it was, was the then 18-year-old Vasiliy Bryukhov from the town of Osa, on the Kama River in the Perm Oblast (administrative division), nearly 1,500km east of

Concealed by the protection of wooded camouflage, T-34 tank commanders gather around a senior instructor who uses wooden or cardboard models to teach battle tactics during a map exercise. Behind them is a Model 1942 T-34. (Thomas Anderson)

Moscow. Called up in September 1941, Bryukhov, to his disappointment, was initially told he would be sent to a ski rifle battalion. He had wanted a posting to a naval school, but instead was sent to a partially completed military camp at Kungur, some 130km east of Osa, where he found himself as part of a working party tasked with completing the camp. The group attended to everything from building dugouts and a mess block to stuffing mattresses with straw and creating stoves from 200-litre drums. With the initial onset of the Russian winter, groups of 12 'trainees' would live in four-man tents, sleeping in their uniforms.

The 'physical fitness' programme undertaken by Bryukhov and his comrades consisted of running from the camp to a nearby forest and then returning with logs. As the forest cleared, the runs became longer. The work teams were offered a bath every three weeks. Sustenance comprised bread, beetroot soup, a form of porridge, potatoes and herrings, but no meat. After a while, a number of the recruits fell ill through malnourishment, cold and exhaustion, but eventually work on the camp was completed and the 'training course' turned to more military matters.

Bryukhov and his hungry young comrades were subjected to several hours of political indoctrination classes, held inside, and drill outside each day. There was also weapons instruction, which involved being taught how to shoot and to assemble and dismantle a rifle and machine gun. Bryukhov came to the conclusion that the more seriously he took the drill, the faster he would be able to escape the camp. It seemed the course leaders approved of such an attitude.

He was then sent for ski training, at which he excelled, and he was made an instructor. In November his ski battalion was sent to Moscow, but on the way their train was subjected to a German air attack and Bryukhov was wounded by a shell splinter in his right knee. After a period of hospitalisation in Perm and another frustrated attempt at being posted to the Navy, Bryukhov was eventually sent as an officer cadet to the Stalingrad tank school in June 1942. A short while later, the city became subjected to enemy bombardment as the German summer offensive got underway.

One morning, it was announced at the daily parade that the school was to be evacuated some 2,000km to the east to the city of Kurgan, where a new training base

Watched by an instructor, the driver of a Model 1942 T-34/76 carefully manoeuvres the tank over a crude but demanding ramp at a training field. (Author's Collection)

was being established. After travelling for five days by train, the tank cadets reached their destination and quickly set up quarters in a school building outside the city. The former headmistress provided her new charges with a regular diet of sweet baked potatoes, which supplemented the standard soup and millet gruel.

Despite exhaustion caused by further malnourishment, training progressed at pace due to the dire war situation facing the Red Army. The cadets were taught the technical aspects of the BT-5 and T-34 designs, as well as the tactical deployment of both tanks. Due to a paucity of the latter, cadets had to practise what they were taught on foot by pretending to be tanks. 'There was only one practical session', Bryukhov wrote. 'I fired three shells and one machine gun magazine.' Aside from that, there was a short period given over to starting and driving a BT-5.

After a month, when it was decided that the cadets had had sufficient training, they were informed by the school commander that although it was appreciated that their 'course' had been expeditious, and that only limited training had been imparted, they would be able to conclude their instruction in action.

Bryukhov was to fare better than many of his comrades, however. In February 1943 he was among 28 of the best cadets selected for a further two months of 'accelerated training'. That being completed, he departed for Chelyabinsk and 7th Reserve Training Tank Regiment. His studies there were interrupted by a brief spell drilling apertures in engine block cylinders at the Kirov Tank Works, after which he was assigned to another reserve tank regiment. Following a further period of platoon and company training, Bryukhov set off on a 50km march to board a train, laden with brand new tanks, that would take him and his fellow freshly-trained tankers to the front. At an unknown point, the train stopped and the tanks and their crews were quickly unloaded. Along with his newly formed battalion, Bryukhov was then marched off to join 99th Brigade of 2nd Tank Corps.

Mikhail Yefimovich Katukov

Embodying the ethos of learning directly from combat, Mikhail Yefimovich Katukov was known for telling his young battalion and company commanders, 'Each battle for us is a school. Analyse, weigh, compare, dissect shortcomings, not just the positive'.

Katukov was born on 17 September, 1900, in a village in the Bolshoe Uvarovo district some 100km from Moscow. His was a peasant family, and so he was put to work as a young boy. But the young Katukov's life would go on to be a military one. At the age of 17 he participated in the October Revolution. By March 1919 he had joined the Red Army, with whom he fought the Whites during the Civil War, and in 1920 he also fought in the Polish–Soviet War. After a solid army career, Katukov had joined the tank arm by 1932, studying to be an officer. At the beginning of World War II, and with the rank of colonel, Katukov was in command of 20th Tank Division, but his unit was equipped with old, unreliable BT-2 and BT-5 light tanks and no new T-34s or KV types.

In mid-August 1941, however, having been recently awarded the Order of the Red Banner, Katukov was summoned to Moscow, where he met with Lieutenant General Yakov Fedorenko, the Red Army's Commander of Tank and Mechanised Forces. Fedorenko informed Katukov that he was to take command of a new tank brigade. Understandably, following a divisional command, Katukov felt a sense of demotion at being given a brigade, but Fedorenko explained that the recent withdrawal of factories to the east of the country and insufficient factory production levels made the formation of anything larger than a brigade impossible. Although Katukov accepted this, he pushed his superior for an assurance that he would receive 50 T-34s for his new brigade.

Based in the Stalingrad area, Katukov set about implementing an efficient and effective training programme for his 4th Tank Brigade. He pressed his commanders and crews to achieve the required levels of skill and tactical understanding, especially in defensive combat, stressing the importance of the awareness of terrain, manoeuvre, the judicious deployment of force strength and the art of deception.

During 1943 at the battle of Kursk, Katukov's principles would be put to the test when his 1st Guards Tank Army

Colonel General Mikhail Yefimovich Katukov was commander of 1st Guards Tank Army from January 1943. His reputation for wiliness and deception earned him the moniker 'General Sly'. For his dynamic command of his Army in the Vistula-Oder offensive in January 1945, Katukov was awarded a second Hero of the Soviet Union Gold Star. (Author's Collection)

suffered badly during the German push in the south. Despite this early attrition, his tactical acumen when it came to battlefield strongpoints, the camouflaging and digging-in of tanks and the timely launching of counter-attacks eventually saw 1st Guards Tank Army inflict heavy losses on the enemy.

Having served in the Vistula–Oder Offensive and the Battle of Berlin, Katukov was awarded the title of Hero of the Soviet Union twice, on 23 September 1944 and 6 April 1945. After the war he commanded Soviet forces in Germany and was appointed Inspector General of the Army. Marshal of the armoured troops Mikhail Katukov passed away in Moscow on 8 June 1976.

COMBAT

In a post-war study on Luftwaffe close air support, the former German air commander General der Flieger a.D. Paul Deichmann wrote 'The 1940 campaign in the West proved that the aeroplane was a most effective weapon against tanks'.

Indeed, one of the earliest examples of how effective the Ju 87 could be occurred in early June 1940 when the Stukas of Hauptmann Hubertus Hitschhold's I./StG 2, operating from Laon-Couvron, attacked a formation of 20–30 French tanks in a wooded area some ten kilometres east-southeast of Roye. The Ju 87s were deployed over two sorties at the request of a small German Panzer and artillery grouping which was struggling to move forward and was blocked by the French armour. The German troops had ascertained that the enemy tanks were preparing to launch an attack to the northwest.

Arriving at the scene shortly after being called up, the first wave of Ju 87s fell into shallow dives and dropped their bombs accurately, causing several of the French tanks to explode and burn. As the Stukas turned back towards Laon-Couvron, they passed low over the Panzers, whose crews, as well as the gunners of the accompanying 88mm guns, waved up to the dive-bombers in appreciation. As the second wave of Ju 87s arrived, it was clear to their crews how effective the earlier work of their comrades had been – the surviving French tanks had pulled back and were scattered over a wide area. This had the effect of making dropping their bombs more difficult, but still there were further successes. As the second wave returned to base, so the dive-bombers flew

Flames and smoke rise up into the sky from the turret and hull of a T-34 on the Russian plain. This would have been what the impact of a well-aimed bomb dropped from a low-level Ju 87 would have looked like. (Thomas Anderson)

through the clouds of dust raised by the renewed advance of the Panzers, and the mobile 88mm guns which flanked them.

It was this kind of action that moulded the tactical cooperation that existed between the Luftwaffe and the Heer on the Eastern Front, where, despite disagreements over its introduction within the Soviet political and military hierarchy, the T-34 went into action for the first time to the west of Grodno, in Byelorussia, soon after the commencement of *Barbarossa*.

Here, on 24 June, the 238 T-34s and 114 KVs of General Mikhail Khatskilevich's 6th Mechanised Corps counter-attacked infantry elements of Generaloberst Hermann Hoth's *Panzergruppe* 3. The German infantry exhausted their ammunition fighting off several attacks by the Soviet tanks, and Ju 87s of VIII.*Fliegerkorps* were called in to clear the path for the German advance. The Stukas duly disrupted and scattered the enemy tanks, and Khatskilevich was killed. As Hoth's *Panzergruppe* advanced on Minsk, so 6th Mechanised Corps became trapped southwest of Grodno at the end of June, resulting in just under a quarter of the Red Army's T-34 strength being lost within days of the German attack.

But the T-34 was desperately needed, for in the summer and autumn of 1941, the better trained, more experienced and better-equipped German Panzer units dominated the Red Army's armoured brigades on the battlefield, the latter equipped as they were with their mostly antiquated and inadequate tanks and their often ill-prepared crews. And, aside from enemy action, frequently Russian tanks would fall victim to engine or mechanical problems, or a lack of ammunition, or flooded engines as a result of novice crews driving them into water.

In one early encounter in Lithuania over 24–25 June 1941, some 50 T-34s from General Alexey Kurkin's 3rd Mechanised Corps engaged advancing armour from 1. and 6.*Panzerdivisions* and did inflict some damage on the enemy. Worryingly for the Germans, they found that their 37mm anti-tank rounds were ineffective against the Russians' frontal armour, and it was only the use of 88mm Flak guns as anti-tank weapons that stopped the T-34s.

Certainly, in the opening months of the invasion, the Ju 87 introduced a new dimension to the battlefield, regularly proving itself as an effective airborne *Panzerjäger* ('tank-hunter'). As German troops advanced deeper into Russia, so the sight of score upon score of shot-up T-34s welcomed them. Often they appeared upside down as if pushed over by some giant hand, or blown up and shattered. Others had simply been abandoned by their frightened crews. This situation is confirmed by the many photographs taken by curious Wehrmacht soldiers who would often pose for snapshots next to the twisted, charred remains of a T-34 by the side of a Russian dirt road or in open country, the victim of Luftwaffe air attack or artillery.

And yet, more astute German commanders would have realised there was a delicate power balance. However many wrecks there were, there always seemed to be replacements, and the appearance of the T-34 meant that existing German tanks had, in essence, become obsolete. Notwithstanding the improvement to the Pz.Kpfw. IV with a longer, high-velocity version of its 75mm gun, the Panzer divisions needed something better, fast.

Furthermore, the T-34 was capable of adversely affecting or interrupting German objectives. On 6 October 1941, the headquarters of General Heinz Guderian's newly redesignated 2.*Panzerarmee* (formerly *Panzergruppe* 2) moved into Sevsk, between

OPPOSITE

Flames rise up from the engine compartment of a T-34/76. When it came to attack from the air, the engine area at the rear where the armour was thin was the most vulnerable part of the tank. As Hans-Ulrich Rudel wrote, 'This is a good spot to aim at because where the engine is, there is always petrol.' (EN Archive)

Bryansk and Rylsk in the area of Army Group Centre. Under cover of Luftwaffe bombers striking at the enemy's line, tanks and motorised infantry from Guderian's formation continued to push eastwards towards the town of Mzensk, on the Zusha river. It was a trap. In the icy mud, Guderian's armour had come up against Colonel Mikhail Katukov's 4th Tank Brigade. Katukov

had skilfully formed a false defensive line and then sucked in around 90 Panzers, against which he deployed the T-34s and KVs of his brigade, as well as more T-34s from 11th Tank Brigade which formed the corps reserve. Guderian wrote how:

> 4th Panzer Division was attacked by Russian tanks to the south of Mzensk and went through some bad hours. This was the first occasion on which the vast superiority of the Russian T-34 to our tanks became plainly apparent. The division suffered grievous casualties. The rapid advance on Tula which we had planned had therefore to be abandoned for the moment.

Ten Panzer III and IVs were lost for half that number of Russian tanks.

In early 1942, following the fighting before Moscow and elsewhere on the Eastern Front, a German report noted that 'the main strength of Russian tanks is not so much their armour generally as the slanted frontal plating. The outstanding manoeuvrability of the T-34 in the field requires special tactical measures [to defeat it], above all the use of terrain safe against tanks'.

As Soviet tank production increased through 1942, so for the Germans there was a corresponding and increasingly urgent need for anti-tank aircraft and appropriate ordnance. With demands on the latter, the Luftwaffe was forced into using heavier 500kg bombs as an emergency measure against tanks. As is often the case with emergency measures, this was not an ideal situation. Tanks were

the smallest and therefore the hardest target to hit for pilots of the Ju 87, but as Oberleutnant Hans-Ulrich Rudel, who would eventually become the most successful of all Stuka anti-tank pilots, wrote, 'Merely to hit a tank is not enough to destroy it'. 'Near misses' were usually ineffective; at most they resulted in temporary immobilisation of a tank as a result of damage to its tracks.

Nevertheless, there had been an entrenched belief that while it *was* recognised that hitting such small targets as tanks in dispersed order was highly difficult, the use of a large-calibre bomb *could* put a tank out of action even if only a 'near hit' was scored. Detonation tests conducted at the Luftwaffe's ordnance *Erprobungsstelle* at Udetfeld, northeast of Beuthen in Upper Silesia, in 1942 firmly contradicted this, however.

Tests were carried out using ten captured T-34s, as well as an American M4 Sherman and three British Churchill Mk IV tanks. The Churchills were found to have the least resilience under attack when an SC 250 bomb was detonated five metres away, the blast breaking apart their armoured shells. By comparison, the T-34s and the Sherman withstood the blast better, even when a similar bomb was detonated just three metres away – the pressure wave from the blast was sufficient to kill the guinea pig test rodents inside the T-34s, as well as setting the diesel fuel in their V-2 engines alight.

A highly respected figure in the Stuka arm, Bruno Lang, was a native of the Sudetenland. He joined the Luftwaffe in March 1936 and was eventually posted to I./St.G 163 in Breslau for dive-bomber training. Subsequently, he took part in the campaigns in Poland, the West and the Balkans. As an oberleutnant, Lang received the Knight's Cross in December 1941 while *Staffelkapitän* of 1./St.G 2. There then followed a stellar career as a Stuka tactician and formation leader culminating in the award of the Swords to the Knight's Cross and Oakleaves on 2 July 1944 whilst he was *Gruppenkommandeur* of III./StG 1. Lang, who ultimately flew 1,008 missions, is seen here on 27 July 1942 following his 600th mission during operations over the Don bend. (EN Archive)

It was accepted that while pressure from a heavier bomb *could* incapacitate a tank if it exploded within three to four metres of a target, it had to detonate immediately above the ground without penetrating the ground first. If the latter occurred, the resulting blast was channelled upwards instead of sideways, producing little damaging effect – something that was understood by Stuka pilot Bruno Lang. A proficient dive-bomber pilot, Lang had flown the Ju 87 over Poland, the West and over Crete before going to Russia with I./StG 2. Of attacking tanks, he wrote:

You always had to keep the same angle of attack, about 45 degrees, and the same release height, and only change it based on the impact of the previous bomb. Releasing too low resulted in a 'delay effect'. The bomb often tore a huge hole in the ground next to the tank, but no shrapnel would hit it. In the best case, it would be damaged and unable to fight for a while. If the approach was too flat, bombs almost always fell ineffectively in a wide arc. Much more successful were attacks on massed tank formations. The result was the destruction of the tanks, the scattering of the [tank] formation and thus the prevention, or at least the delay, of their attack. In addition, the attacking spirit and intent of the tank crews was reduced. Attack with the standard two-gun fixed armament was only successful in the rarest of cases as a result of accidental strikes through the ventilation slots on the plates above the engine. Results were better if the tanks carried external fuel canisters for longer journeys.

The tests at Udetfeld led ordnance engineers and Luftwaffe weapons specialists to conclude that to efficiently destroy a tank, much smaller *Streubomben* (incendiary scatter bombs) would be needed so that amongst a large number of tanks, the chances of a direct hit was increased. To ensure armour penetration, such bombs would need to carry hollow-charge warheads, but the Luftwaffe required that they be capable of penetrating 100mm of armoured steel, while also creating splinter blast against crew as well as Russian infantry who frequently rode on tanks or followed them in close proximity during attacks. Thus, there was a need for a new kind of anti-tank bomb. It would not arrive until early 1944.

In the meantime, provided the ordnance was available, which it usually was, according to the *Geschwaderkommodore* of StG 2, Major Paul-Werner Hozzel, the standard load carried by his unit's Ju 87s for an anti-tank sortie would be one 500kg bomb with an armour-piercing head, or one 250kg *Flammbomb* (an incendiary bomb with a warhead of 30 per cent petrol and 70 per cent crude oil), or three 250kg armour-piercing bombs, one each mounted below the fuselage and each wing. Sometimes a load would combine a *Flammbomb* and two armour-piercing bombs.

It was standard operational procedure to release bombs individually against a formation of tanks, but without delay, and often at the lowest possible altitude. When deployed in *Ketten* of three aircraft, attacks would be made from different directions once close to the target.

During Operation *Blau*, launched on 28 June 1942, the Ju 87s of StG 2 flew continuous missions from dawn to dusk in support of the armoured spearheads of Army Group B advancing on Voronezh. Hozzel recalled:

FLAMMBOMB AND SC 250 BOMBS

A single 250kg *Flammbomb* could be carried on the centreline *Schloß* 500/XII C rack, this incendiary bomb being fitted with a warhead comprising 30 per cent petrol and 70 per cent crude oil. Ju 87Ds so equipped usually paired the *Flammbomb* with a single SC 250 on racks under each outer wing.

Ju 87Ds of the *Gruppenstab* II./StG 2 carry out a low-level bombing attack on Soviet T-34s around Kalach, in the Don bend, during the German summer offensive in August 1942. The Stukas formed an integral part of the German advance towards the Volga and the city of Stalingrad, providing air support for Generalfeldmarschall Friedrich Paulus' Sixth Army. 'We had been flying sorties again and again', wrote the Kommodore of StG 2, Oberstleutnant Paul-Werner Hozzel, 'day after day, from morning to night, ahead of our armoured divisions which were advancing rapidly to the south, keeping in constant contact with them by radio'. The aircraft dropped a mixture of 250kg and 500kg bombs. As an evasive manoeuvre, the T-34s would endeavour to disperse or weave as much as they could. The dust of the Russian plains was a hindrance to the dive-bomber pilots' visibility and made the process of targeting highly difficult.

The landscape was flat and easy to survey, with small villages and low cottages scattered here and there, some wooded areas between brooks and small rivers – the ideal terrain for tanks. Our own tanks had their front plates covered with black-white-red material so that we could, at any time, easily spot our spearheads. Moreover, we communicated with each other via ground–air and air–ground recognition signals. To this end, we had special ammunition and signal flares which we could fire through an opening in the cockpit if we wanted to ask the ground troops to mark the frontline or to indicate enemy targets by ground signal.

At this stage the advance of German ground forces was so rapid that StG 2 had to transfer by 'jumps' of as far as 300km or more from one airfield to another.

In mid-July Hozzel was given a composite command made up of I. and II./StG 2, II./StG 1 and I./StG 76 – some 170 Ju 87s in all, along with 12 Bf 110s of a reconnaissance *Staffel* assigned to StG 2 and an Italian unit of 15 Macchi C.200 fighters. The *Gruppen* of StG 2 flew into Tatsinskaya from Akhtyrka on 20 July.

Conditions at the airfield, lying around 150km west of Stalingrad, but east of the Donets, were typically rudimentary. Personnel entrenched themselves in bunkers – a difficult job, given the sun-baked hardness of the ground – or in tents that were more vulnerable to enemy air attack. Some aircraft were able to be parked in crude revetments, but most were simply left in the open. Serviceability was at around 70 per cent, and therefore the *Geschwader* was able to fly combat missions with about 120 Stukas on a maximum-strength mission, for which they could expect VIII.*Fliegerkorps* to also arrange fighter and/or *Zerstörer* escort. Hozzel recalled that there were no logistic problems at this time, with fuel, ammunition and bombs being delivered by rail and truck.

Shortly after the war, Oberst Hubertus Hitschhold, an experienced dive-bomber pilot who was appointed *General der Schlachtflieger* in November 1943, summarised the command principles used by Ju 87 units (and other types) at this time:

> For operations by anti-tank units, ground and air defence were especially considered, but weather conditions were of less importance. Even in very bad weather with very low ceilings, anti-tank units could carry out effective and successful raids. Missions for anti-tank units were flown only against special centres of resistance at the front. Because of the mobility of tanks, finding them in a short space of time was often hard. Especially in obscure situations, accurate reports about the appearance of tanks and details of their locations were seldom available. The operations of anti-tank units therefore usually took place in a free-sweep attack, in which the aircraft first had to find the tanks in a large target area. Therefore, training in recognition of tanks was especially important for the anti-tank flyers.

This was the theory, but it was easier said than done. By late summer, the conditions on the vast Russian battlefields had become extremely difficult for the Ju 87s. On 25 August 1942, Hauptmann Herbert Pabst of StG 77 noted in his diary:

> The whole countryside is veiled in a thick dust haze – you have to climb to about 2,000m to reach the clearer air. Over the battle area, the cloud of smoke and dust from the

moving tanks and troop columns and from the fires and explosions is so thick that it's extremely difficult to find your way or locate the target. You see tanks crawling over the Steppe: are they ours – or theirs? It is so difficult, and so important to make sure.

By this stage, the Ju 87 units were informing their pilots on the 'art' of identifying and destroying Soviet tanks by using large cardboard and wooden models. 'We are taught where the most vulnerable parts are located', wrote Oberleutnant Hans-Ulrich Rudel, the *Staffelkapitän* of 1./StG 2, 'engine, petrol tank, ammunition chamber'.

Indeed, in one mid-war memo issued to the Luftwaffe anti-tank units, among the required prerequisites for combat were 'exact knowledge of the construction of a tank, of the strengths of its walls, of the location of its ammunition containers and fuel tanks, the engine, and above all of its vulnerable spots'. Again – easier said than done.

The problem was compounded by the fact that throughout the second half of 1941 and during 1942, the Russians had found that the Luftwaffe made a prime target of their railway network. As a result, when T-34s were delivered to the front by train, they were carefully encased in 'walls' of straw bales and then covered with tarpaulins in order to give the impression from the air that the train was laden with farm produce. But Luftwaffe dive-bomber pilots quickly learned to see through this ruse.

The Russians also became adept at deception. Dummy tanks were built in large numbers, made and painted to resemble T-34s, in order to draw wasted attacks from German ground-attack aircraft. The dummies were usually constructed of wooden frames covered with heavy fabric, and some had wooden sides, but others were made from earth, snow and logs. These were assembled by tank crews overseen by officers who had received specialist training. On one occasion, in another form of deception, a formation of Ju 87s attacked a column of tractors that had been camouflaged as tanks in the marshalling yards at Smolensk.

'Real' T-34s, meanwhile, had made not only an impression on the Germans, but also on senior Russian officers who mattered. One was the commander of 1st Tank Corps, Major General Mikhail Katukov. On 17 September 1942, a

Hauptmann Hans-Ulrich Rudel (left), the most renowned of all Luftwaffe anti-tank pilots, checks a list of 'Main Types' of Soviet tanks while his radio operator/gunner, Oberfeldwebel Erwin Hentschel, holds a cardboard recognition model of a Russian KV-2 heavy assault tank, and the man behind holds a similar model of a T-34. This photograph was probably taken at the time Rudel was in command of III./StG 2 from the summer of 1943. He used such models to instruct and familiarise his pilots. (EN Archive)

Taken from a Red Army manual captured by German forces, this illustration shows troops concealing what appears to be a T-34/85 on a railway flatbed wagon by means of 'walls' of straw bales and a tarpaulin top sheet. This ruse was used to hide and protect tanks from German air attack. (Author's Collection)

wary Katukov was ordered to report to Stalin in the Kremlin. The Soviet leader wanted to know how Russian tanks were performing on the Bryansk Front, and what opinions Katukov held about them. The major general replied that 'the T-34 fully acquitted itself in battle, and the tankers put great trust in it. But the heavy KV and the combat vehicles T-60 and T-70 are not liked'.

Stalin wanted to know why. 'The KV, comrade Stalin', Katukov answered, 'is very heavy, slow-moving and, as you know, unmanoeuvrable. They overcome obstacles with great difficulty, while the T-34s do it with ease. KVs break bridges and generally cause unnecessary troubles. And the armament of the 76mm gun is the same as that on the T-34. So what's the combat advantage of a heavy tank?'

Katukov was promptly given command of the new 3rd Mechanised Corps.

Throughout September 1942, the weather remained warm and dry in central and southern Russia. StG 2 was rendering continual support to 6.*Armee* as it advanced towards Stalingrad, across the Chir towards Kalach in the Don bend. It was over the flat plains west of Kalach that the *Geschwader* encountered, for the first time, a very large concentration of Soviet tanks – what the *Geschwaderkommodore*, Major Hozzel, described as a 'tank barrier'.

The tactic used by the Stukas to counter this was to continually have one *Staffel* of nine to 12 aircraft in contact with the enemy armour. As one *Staffel* pressed home its attack, the next was already approaching the area of engagement. By adopting such unrelenting measures, it meant that the Soviet tank crews were distracted and therefore denied the opportunity to concentrate on the ground-fighting against German tanks. Hozzel would often lead his formations in the air, and he recalled of this particular time:

I cannot remember how many tanks faced us. It may have been 200 of them, or even more. We saw many packs of T-34s, also some older types. The fronts between friend and foe were clearly discernible. It would have been pointless to attack in larger groups because our aircraft would have hindered one another. Instead, we detailed one *Staffel* after another. They approached single tanks in *Ketten* and from the side, from south to north, or vice versa. Each aircraft looked for its target, flying parallel to its neighbour, at approach angles of 30 to 40 degrees, aiming with the whole aircraft through the reflex sight at the centre of the tank, then dropping 500kg bombs with tank-busting heads into the tank's side while making an extremely low pass above the ground. *Flammbomben* also proved to be most effective because due to the heat developing, the crew was incapacitated when the tank's fuel storage exploded.

It was, of course, imperative to react rapidly, to pull one's aircraft up in a split second after dropping the bomb, then to fly across the tank so as to avoid being hit by the explosion of our own bomb. It sounds adventurous, and that's exactly what it was.

Equally, in the smoke and haze of battle on the ground, amidst the noise and lurching movement of tank-versus-tank combat, to command a T-34 in action was a frantic job, as Vasiliy Bryukhov described from his experience of fighting at Kursk in July 1943:

A smoke-charred STZ-manufactured T-34 sits abandoned in a city somewhere in southern Russia in 1942–43. The tank has cast road wheels and what appears to be a simplified turret intended for ease of manufacture. Note also the lack of fixtures on the hull. Heat from fire seems to have wrinkled the thin engine grille frame. (Author's Collection)

You are on the move, you look for targets, you shoot, you spin around. A T-34/76 commander works like a circus artist – he lays the gun, he shoots, he gives orders to his gun loader and driver, he gets in touch with other tanks from the platoon via radio. This requires his full concentration, otherwise in combat he is done for.

Thus the 'distraction' of air attack, let alone its effect, was very much unwelcome. As an evasive manoeuvre, if the crew of a T-34 spotted a Ju 87 coming in for an attack, they would immediately start to turn their tank – but this would often make a bad situation worse, as Hozzel described:

Seeing as pretty well any Soviet tank crew must have felt that they were being attacked along the whole width of our formations' offensive front, our tank-hunting strikes obviously had quite a paralysing effect on the capability of the enemy and his firepower. I should not fail to mention that among the Russian tanks there were also anti-aircraft tanks we had to watch out for. They were easily identifiable by their vertical barrels. It goes without saying that we would attack them first. But some of them fired from camouflaged positions and we couldn't make them out in time. Still, they were not able to score hits on our Ju 87s, which attacked at a slanted dive angle. The speed of our aircraft was too great for their cannon to follow us.

One Russian practice was to clear damaged tanks from the battlefield quickly so that, wherever possible, they could be restored to working order. After sunset Soviet troops would immediately set about their task, even in bad weather. Parts for repairs were also salvaged from badly damaged tanks. Sometimes parts were improvised on the spot from scrap materials. Thus, as Rudel emphasised, Ju 87 pilots soon learned that enemy tanks had to be seen to be *definitively* destroyed to ensure that they would be eliminated from future operations.

61

Red Army infantry in snow smocks move up towards Stalingrad from the south on the backs of T-34s in February 1943. Despite exhaust fumes, those men at the rear of the tanks must have benefited from the warmth of the engines. (Getty Images)

A 37mm BK 3.7 cannon fitted for static firing tests beneath the port wing of a Ju 87G. The weapon's outer breech cover has been removed, and thus the photograph offers a good view of the breech construction. The void port for the wing gun mount in the wing leading edge has been covered. (EN Archive)

The tank barrier at Kalach was finally broken under the combined and coordinated operations of the Heer and the Luftwaffe. The way to Stalingrad lay ahead. Panzer units crossed the Don on a wide front while continuing to receive close air support from StG 2, while StG 77 did likewise in the Kuban. Within days, the armoured spearheads of 6.*Armee* entered Stalingrad from the north and south, but it soon became apparent that a tough contest lay ahead for the capture of the city.

In November 1942, a flight by a Ju 88 conducting 'strategic reconnaissance' of the railways north of the Don bend picked up significant quantities of Soviet armour, as reported by the intelligence officer of VIII.*Fliegerkorps*. 'On the wide southward road

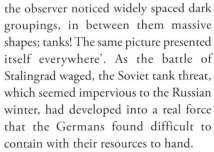

the observer noticed widely spaced dark groupings, in between them massive shapes; tanks! The same picture presented itself everywhere'. As the battle of Stalingrad waged, the Soviet tank threat, which seemed impervious to the Russian winter, had developed into a real force that the Germans found difficult to contain with their resources to hand.

However, a new weapon for the Ju 87 to fight the threat with was under development. According to Bruno Lang, 'only with the appearance of the Ju 87 equipped with two 3.7cm anti-tank cannon could we really speak of successful combat. The bombing of tanks that had already broken through our own positions was impossible without endangering our own troops, but they could always be fought very successfully with cannon'.

As early as February 1942, the *Erprobungsstelle* at Rechlin had been investigating the use of 3.7cm armour-piercing, tungsten carbide-cored, HE ammunition. Trials had shown that with such a shell (*Hartemunition*) 85mm in length and 16mm in diameter, armoured steel 120mm thick (equating to a strength of 80kg/mm^2) could be wholly penetrated from a range of 100m and at an angle of 60 degrees. This made the prospect of using a 3.7cm gun as a ground-attack weapon an attractive proposition, and so Luftwaffe ballistics engineers went to work on producing what became the 37mm *Bordkanone* 3.7 automatic cannon, a development based on the 3.7cm Flak 18 anti-aircraft gun built by Rheinmetall in 1935. The BK 3.7 measured 3.75m in length and weighed 275kg. The rate of fire was 140 rounds per minute at a velocity of 860m per second. A magazine with six shells weighed 12.5kg.

In January 1943, a Ju 87D-1 was sent to Rechlin and then to the Eastern Front to trial the fitment of two underwing BK 3.7, each gun mounted outboard of the undercarriage leg. Under the supervision of the 1. and 2.*Staffeln* of the *Versuchskommando für Panzerbekämpfung* (Test Command for Anti-Tank Warfare) led by Oberstleutnant Otto Weiß, tests were carried out at Rechlin and then in Russia against captured Red Army tanks by a core of pilots that included Hauptmann Hans-Karl Stepp, Oberleutnante Hans-Ulrich Rudel and Günther Jacoby and Feldwebel Hans Ludwig. Results were generally encouraging, but Rudel was circumspect and wrote later:

Static firing tests of a 37mm BK 3.7 cannon being conducted with Ju 87G GS+MD, which has been raised using a hydraulic jack then supported forward by trestles and tensioned stanchions from the wings. The guns appear to have been fired recently judging by the smoke and dust haze in the target pit. The sign above warns, 'Risk of death! Entry to the shooting range is strictly forbidden for all unauthorised personnel'. (EN Archive)

ENGAGING THE ENEMY

The pilot of a Ju 87G manouevres his aircraft in low behind a T-34 and opens fire with his 37mm BK 3.7 cannon. According to Oberst Hans-Ulrich Rudel, the fumes from a tank's exhaust would betray its presence. It was found that an attack against the rear of the tank, where much of its surface area was not armoured and where the engine and fuel pipes were housed, resulted in success. As Rudel wrote, 'This is a good spot to aim at because where the engine is, there is always petrol'. The cartridge of a 37mm shell weighed 1.460kg, to which was added a projectile weight of 0.62kg, explosive at 0.09kg and a case weight of 0.61kg. The rate of fire was 140 rounds per minute at a velocity of 860m per second. A magazine with six shells weighed 12.5kg.

The Ju 87, which is not too fast, now becomes even slower and unfavourably affected by the load of the cannon it carries. Its manoeuvrability is disadvantageously reduced and its landing speed is increased considerably. But now armament potency is a prime consideration over flying performance.

While it was recognised that there was some compromise in handling and performance as a result of the cannon installation, it was not considered adverse enough not to proceed with further operational development.

The Ju 87G-1 emerged in early 1943 initially as a specialist tank-destroyer rebuilt from the Ju 87D-3 dive-bomber. Most of the short-winged conversions, of which 34 examples were produced, were delivered to the *Vers. Kdo. für Pz. Bekämpfung* which, by February, was operating in the Bryansk area. These were followed by the first series G-1s in April. The variant was powered by a Junkers Jumo 211J liquid-cooled engine that gave the aircraft a maximum speed of 400km/h and a range of 2,000km.

A BK 3.7cm was suspended beneath each wing of a Ju 87G-1 to fire outside of the propeller arc, thus eliminating the need for synchronisation. The breech mechanism was housed in a streamlined pod fitted to braces just outboard of the wing crank. The pod, which extended approximately three-quarters the width of the wing, aided aerodynamics and gave protection to the breech from dust and combat damage. Above and to the front of the pod, extending slightly over the rear of the barrel, was another smaller faired pod which housed the weapon's hydraulic oil heater and air intake.

The cannon were fed by six-round clips, with two clips accommodated in metal hinged trays loaded horizontally into each gun, each tray extending to either side after fitment, thus giving one aircraft 24 rounds to fire. The empty shell cases were not ejected but fed back into the clip on the opposite side of the gun and then removed after the aircraft had landed. The low ammunition load meant that missions were generally of short duration and inefficient in terms of fuel consumption. When the cannon and magazines were fitted to a Ju 87G-1 all other bomb racks under the fuselage were removed, thus making it a dedicated cannon-armed *Panzerjäger*. The cannon were aimed using a remotely-operated pneumatic sighting system.

Units known to have flown the G variant included 10.(Pz.)*Staffel*/StG 1

Classic view of a Ju 87G as it turns, engine running, in a cloud of dust. The aircraft carries the emblem of a T-34 on its nose, denoting its specialist anti-tank role, as well as tactical markings on its wheel spat. The Stuka is probably a machine belonging to either the *Versuchskommando für Panzerbekämpfung* or 10.(Pz.)/SG 2. The T-34 silhouette marking was applied to several such aircraft, including at one point the Ju 87 flown by Hauptmann Hans-Ulrich Rudel. (EN Archive)

(10.(Pz)/SG 77 from 18 October 1943), 10.(Pz.)/StG 2 (10.(Pz)/SG 2 from 18 October 1943), 10.(Pz.)/SG 3 (formed from 4./StG 2 in February 1944, it became 3.(Pz.)/SG 9 on 7 January 1945) and 10.(Pz.)/SG 77 (formed from 10.(Pz.)/StG 1 on 18 October 1943, it became 10.(Pz.)/SG 1 on 27 January 1944). 'On paper', each *Panzer Staffel* fielded a strength of 12 BK 3.7cm-armed Ju 87Gs in addition to four bomb-carrying aircraft intended to suppress defensive fire from enemy anti-aircraft batteries.

After introduction in numbers, results with the BK 3.7cm-equipped Junkers did vary, and some units found the weapon to be unsatisfactory. Thus, they removed the cannon and returned to carrying bombs. But those crews which prevailed began to devise effective short-dive or shallow glide, low-level attack tactics in which an enemy tank was approached in a long, straight run, and fire opened at the closest possible range. Proof of the success of this method came in July 1943 when, despite his earlier reservations, Hauptmann Rudel of StG 2 destroyed 12 T-34s in one day, each kill being recorded by a photograph. However, of the introduction of the Ju 87G into service, Rudel remembered:

Oberleutnant Andreas Kuffner (second from right) in conversation with fellow pilots of 10.(Pz)/SG 3 in 1944. Kuffner was awarded the Knight's Cross on 16 April 1943 in recognition of his 600 operational missions. A former Flak gunner, he took pilot training and flew exclusively in the East where, during an eventual total of 700 missions, he was credited with the destruction of some 60 Soviet tanks. Awarded the Oakleaves on 20 December 1944, Kuffner was killed on 30 April 1945 while *Kommandeur* of I.(Pz)/SG 9 when his aircraft was attacked by Allied fighters as he attempted to land. (EN Archive)

The outlook is none too rosy. We are the object of commiseration wherever we appear, and our sympathisers do not predict a long lease of life for any of us. The heavier the Flak, the quicker my tactics develop. It is obvious that we must always carry bombs to deal with the enemy defence. But we cannot carry them on our cannon-carrying aircraft as the bomb load makes them too heavy. Besides, it is no longer possible to go into a dive with a cannon-carrying Ju 87 because the strain on the wings is too great. The practical answer is therefore to have an escort of normal Stukas.

The evolved standard procedures were to fire at a tank's side armour, where the BK 3.7cm was effective, or to aim for the thinner armour at the rear of a tank where the engine vents were located. Even if this could not be done, a tank could be immobilised by blowing off a track tread.

The introduction of the Ju 87G compelled some Russian tank commanders to let off smoke cannisters fitted to their tanks in attempts to simulate destruction, but the more experienced anti-tank pilots such as Rudel knew that a genuinely destroyed tank burned with flames. A hit tank would often explode instantaneously if fire broke out close to its store of ammunition, and so for a Ju 87 flying at an altitude of just five to ten metres above it, the situation could be, as Rudel described it, 'uncomfortable'. He experienced personally such a scenario on two occasions in his first few days of flying the Ju 87G in combat.

Under operational conditions it was found that a 3.7cm cannon round could penetrate 58mm of armour at a range of 100m at 60 degrees.

As the Ju 87G-1 went into service, so the Junkers works at Bremen-Lemwerder commenced construction of 208 new G-2s based on a conversion from the longer-spanned Ju 87D-5, which gave more strength and stability to the cannon installation. Cold weather heaters were later installed in some cannon to enable continued operations in the Russian winter. The G-2 reached frontline units in early 1944.

An armourer prepares to load a clip of six high-explosive 37mm rounds into the covered outboard metal ammunition tray on the side of the faired breech pod of a BK 3.7cm gun. The hinged door to the tray is open and the Stuka's wheel spats have been removed to prevent clogging from dust and clumps of earth. (EN Archive)

As the fighting on the Eastern Front ebbed and flowed for the Germans, there was no doubt that the anti-tank Stukas were being called upon increasingly as a 'fire brigade'. For example, on 20 February 1943 at StG 2's headquarters in Nikolajev, Major Hozzel took a call from Generalfeldmarschall Wolfram Freiherr von Richthofen, the commander of *Luftflotte* 4, who asked how many Ju 87s could be made operationally ready at short notice. The aircraft were needed urgently to beat off strong Soviet forces threatening the Dnipro front. Hozzel informed von Richthofen that he could muster 46 aircraft and crews ready for take-off within the hour. Von Richthofen ordered him to transfer immediately to Dnipropetrovsk, where the *Geschwader* would function under General der Flieger Kurt Pflugbeil's IV. *Fliegerkorps*.

Once again Hozzel was also given command of an ad hoc *Gefechtsverband*, which comprised the aircraft of his own *Geschwader* plus around 80 Ju 87s of StG 77. Hozzel recalls:

I was commander of a mixed *Geschwader* of about 125 aircraft. All of them were thrown into battle as fighter-bombers for close air support of the Army on the battlefield. We flew our low-level attacks in regular style, from morning to evening, with bombs and with fire from our aircraft armament against the Russian divisions attacking in the open field, and also against artillery positions. But strangely enough, we hardly noticed any tanks. We had a feeling they were operating only at night when we could not fly, and so presented no danger. We did spot a few of them, well camouflaged, under haystacks and in barns. Their wheel tracks betrayed them.

The miraculous happened. Once again the Army succeeded, with our support, in stopping the advance of the Red Army on that section of the front, and even repulsed it to the Barvenkovo area. The frontlines seemed to be stabilised again.

By 1943, the 76mm F-34 gun on the Red Army's T-34 was ageing and unable to damage the glacis armour of the German Panther at a range beyond 300m, but the

T-34 brigades could rely on an operational readiness of between 70–90 per cent at any one time, whereas the German Panther achieved just 35 per cent. This was the situation at the time of Operation *Zitadelle*, the last great German offensive on the Eastern Front, aimed at sealing off the 150km-wide by 65km-deep Soviet thrust between Orel in the north and Belgorod in the south, centred on the city of Kursk. The skies above what became a titanic battle of armour at Kursk in July saw, simultaneously, the twilight of the Ju 87 in its classic dive-bombing role and its emergence as an adapted but effective cannon-bearing anti-tank aircraft.

When it came to attacking a T-34 or other type of Russian tank, Rudel described the methodology as follows:

> We have always to try to hit a tank in one of its most vulnerable places. The front is always the strongest part of every tank; therefore every tank invariably tries as far as possible to offer its front to the enemy. Its sides are less strongly protected. But the best target for us is the stern. It is there that the engine is housed, and the necessity for cooling this power centre permits only a thin armour plating. In order to further assist the cooling, this plating is perforated with large holes. This is a good spot to aim at because where the engine is, there is always petrol. When its engine is running a tank is easily recognisable from the air by the blue fumes of the exhaust. On its sides, the tank carries petrol and ammunition. But there the armour is stronger than at the back.

In the southern sector of the *Zitadelle* offensive, the efforts of II.SS-*Panzer-Korps* were bolstered considerably by Ju 87 *Staffeln*. In these operations Rudel and his fellow pilots in the specialist cannon *Staffeln* were also aided by the medium green camouflage of the T-34s set against the baked yellow of the Steppe grass, helping to make the tanks highly visible targets.

Indeed, time and again during the battle at Kursk, the Ju 87s – cannon-armed and bomb-carrying – came to the aid of their Panzer comrades. As just one example, on 9 July in the area of XLVIII.*Panzerkorps*, the armoured reconnaissance battalion of the *Panzer-Grenadier Division 'Grossdeutschland'* was blocked in its attempt to approach what was referenced as Point 260.8. Ju 87s came to the unit's aid, as recounted in the divisional history:

> The attack was preceded by Stuka attacks on what appeared to be enemy armoured spearheads and troop concentrations farther to the north. Waves of dive-bombers dropped their loads with precision on the Russian tanks. Under the cover of this really outstanding air support, the battle group of the Armoured Reconnaissance Battalion approached point 260.8.

A Ju 87D of II./StG 2 is bombed up in readiness for another mission in the summer of 1943. The armourers have just used a hydraulic lift to attach a 500kg bomb to the centreline rack, while a pair of 250kg incendiaries hang from the outer wing racks. The man in the cockpit, who appears to be the pilot, is testing the control surfaces. The aircraft is adorned with the red version of the mounted knight emblem of StG 2, denoting that this Stuka is from 5.*Staffel*. Note the *Staffel* colour has also been applied to the spinner tip. (EN Archive)

Returning to base, where the aircraft were quickly refuelled and rearmed, the Stukas then flew back to the frontline to facilitate *'Grossdeutschland's'* advance, providing further support throughout the day until nightfall. The following day, Ju 87s worked closely with elements of 1.SS-*Panzer-Grenadier Division 'Leibstandarte Adolf Hitler'* and 3.SS-*Panzer-Grenadier Division 'Totenkopf'*, bombing and firing cannon at T-34s as soldiers from the *Waffen*-SS battled to secure bridgeheads over the River Psel and at Hill 222.6.

On 12 July, as Soviet and German tank formations clashed in the notorious engagement at Prokhorovka, the Ju 87s of StG 2 and StG 77 carried out their lowest number of daily sorties since the beginning of the battle of Kursk – 150 in all. This compares with no fewer than 447 the day before and 1,071 on 5 July. Despite this, it was during one day in this week-long period of intense action that Rudel, while flying one of his initial sorties in the Ju 87G, destroyed four tanks. By day's end he had accounted for another eight along the front of II.SS-*Panzerkorps*. As he wrote with some grandiloquence in his memoirs, 'In the first attack four tanks explode under the hammer blows of my cannons; by the evening the total rises to 12. We are all seized with a kind of passion for the chase from the glorious feeling of having saved much German bloodshed with every tank destroyed'.

A bomb-pocked wintry Russian landscape as a result of German air attack against Red Army tanks in the winter of 1943–44, the ground a maze of tank tracks. German aerial reconnaissance analysts have marked what are probably the locations of wrecked or abandoned vehicles or guns. (Author's Collection)

The battle at Kursk inflicted heavy casualties on both sides. In the south, Lieutenant-General Pavel Rotmistrov's 5th Guards Tank Army had more than 400 tanks knocked out in the first two days of the fighting at Prokhorovka. Although mechanics worked around the clock to bring as many as 112 tanks back to operational readiness, by 19 July the army still had 180 requiring repairs. But the point was that unlike German losses, the Russians had managed to restore the army's strength to 503 tanks and 40 self-propelled guns by the 30th.

Rudel is purported to have destroyed more than 519 enemy tanks alone by war's end, making him the 'ace' of anti-tank aces. In the last weeks of the war, despite privations, Generaloberst Ferdinand Schörner, an army group commander on what remained of the Eastern Front, so recognised Rudel's contribution in the war against Soviet armour that whenever the Ju 87 pilot arrived at his headquarters he would present him with a cake 'usually in the shape of a T-34 covered in sugar icing', Rudel recalled, 'and the number, whatever it was at the time, of tanks I was credited with'.

There were other aces. For example, Oberleutnant Wilhelm Bromen, who flew Ju 87s with 4./StG 2, is credited with destroying 76 tanks, and Oberfeldwebel Werner Honsberg of 1./StG 77 has 30 to his name, while Feldwebel Josef Blümel is recorded as destroying 60 tanks flying the Ju 87G with 10.(Pz)/SG 3. All these pilots were decorated with the Knight's Cross.

By mid-1943, despite becoming increasingly vulnerable to Soviet fighters, which were being built in increasing numbers, the Ju 87 could still pack a punch. Fighting to defend Kharkov on 20 August, General Erhard Raus, commander of the battered remnants of 11.*Armeekorps* that had been hurriedly reinforced by 156 Panthers, Tigers and *Sturmgeschütz* IIIs from 2.SS *Panzer-Division*, observed yet again the Luftwaffe's Stukas in action after they were called in to target the Red Army's westwards advance.

As the Ju 87s went about their work, dropping heavy ordnance, Raus observed how 'dark fountains of earth erupted skyward and were followed by heavy thunderclaps and shocks that resembled an earthquake'. With the villages in which the T-34s had been concealed left in flames after the Junkers had done their work, the Russian tanks rolled forward across the cornfields and slammed into the German armour. By the end of the day, no fewer than 184 T-34s had been lost.

In the spring of 1944 the Soviet tank arm and the Luftwaffe each introduced a new weapon to their arsenals. On the Soviet side, the T-34 needed to be up-gunned to take account of the German Tiger, Panther and *Jagdpanzer* types. While the tested and proven T-34/76 would remain in service to the end of the war, a new T-34/85 medium tank began to equip the Guards' tank brigades from around this time, although ultimately not all tank units received the new model.

Koshkin's successor as head of the T-34 design bureau, Alexander Aleksandrovich Morozov, was an experienced engineer who had designed the tank's diesel engine. In the summer of 1943, Morozov produced a revised design which saw the introduction of a new turret fitted with a D-5T 85mm gun, making it comparable to the

KV-85 heavy tank and SU-85 self-propelled gun. The D-5T (T for 'tank') was adapted from the D-5 anti-aircraft gun and Morozov fitted it into a modified, larger KV-85 turret that could accommodate a crew of five. The result was a tank with a gun that could penetrate the front armour of a Tiger at 1,000m and which, defensively, benefited from increased 75mm frontal armour. The increase in the number of crew also took away some of the tasks which had burdened the commander. However, the new gun was 400kg heavier, had more limited elevation and came with a low rate of fire – only five to eight rounds per minute.

Following the 1943 Model was the 1944 Model, which carried a ZiS-S-53 85mm gun produced by Vasiliy Grabin at the TsAKB Artillery Design Bureau within the Josef Stalin Zavod No. 92 at Gorky, as well as refined internal accommodation and improved equipment, including the gunner's sight and a turret radio, which had previously been housed in the hull. Major General Katukov described how 'the design of the T-34 with powerful new armament infused us with optimism and reinforced us psychologically. We could hardly wish for anything more'.

The final 1945 Model featured an electrically-powered turret and a larger cupola for the commander.

Meanwhile, on 5 March 1944, Hitler personally gave approval for the introduction of the new hollow-charge SD-4-HL *Splitterbombe* for ground-attack aircraft. Weighing just four kilogrammes, the bomb was fitted with an eAZ (66) super-fast impact fuse and was intended for deployment primarily by Ju 87s against tanks, but also other tracked vehicles, as well as troops and unarmoured targets. A load of 74 SD-4-HLs could be dropped from an AB 500-1 *Abwurfbehälter* (air-drop container), the combined weight of which (with container) totalled around 400kg. The bombs were manufactured in either moulded, cast or tempered steel or cast iron.

Tests at Udetfeld conducted over a year had shown that in order to set fire to the fuel or ammunition of two tanks out of a group of four within an area 18 x 24m, a scatter dropping pattern would be needed with the aim of hitting each tank with two SD-4-HL bombs. The only problem crews came across was that the doors on the AB 500 did not open wide enough to allow a sufficient scatter.

In the spring of 1944, as German forces fell back inexorably across the Eastern Front, a grave loss to the *Sturzkampfflieger* occurred on 30 April when Major Alwin Boerst, *Gruppenkommandeur* of I./StG 2, was killed. Flying a Ju 87G-1, possibly for the first time, on a *Panzerjagd* close to the village of Pîrliţa, northeast of Jassy in Romania, Boerst, as always, attacked the first tanks despite strong defensive ground fire. The T-34s were positioned close to the Pîrliţa-Jassy railway line, and as he flew in at low

Soviet infantry ride on the hulls of T-34/85 Model 1944 tanks. The 85mm Zis-S-53 main gun was effective against German tanks and self-propelled guns up to a range of 1,000m. This model also included an improved gunner's sight and, as part of overall enhanced internal layout, the radio was relocated from the front hull to the turret. Zavod Nos. 183, 112 and 174 produced 10,632 T-34/85s in 1944 and a further 5,959 in the first six months of 1945. (Thomas Anderson)

Ju 87Ds from 1./SG 1 fly another mission over the frozen and forested terrain of central Russia in early 1944, after which I.*Gruppe* pulled back to eastern Poland. Each aircraft carries a 500kg bomb on its centreline rack, while visible under their wings are *Abwurfbehälter* (AB) 500 weapons containers loaded with 4kg SD-4-HL fragmentation bombs. The aircraft have been given a rough overall winter 'whitewash', although the individual letter 'F' in white of the machine nearest to the camera (L1+FH) can be clearly seen on the wing underside. (EN Archive)

level to engage them his aircraft was hit by Flak. The Ju 87 caught fire and became uncontrollable. VAlthough his radio operator/rear gunner Oberfeldwebel Ernst Filius was able to climb out of the stricken Junkers, his parachute became caught on its tail. Despite having managed to halt the enemy advance, Boerst and Filius were killed. They were buried in a common grave. Boerst was awarded the Swords to his Knight's Cross posthumously on 6 April 1944, having flown more than 1,500 missions, while Filius received the Knight's Cross on 19 May, having completed in excess of 1,000 missions.

On 23 June 1944, the Soviets launched Operation *Bagration*, designed to liberate Byelorussia and to destroy as much of the German Army Group Centre as possible, paving the way into Poland. As historian Anthony Tucker-Jones has aptly described it, *Bagration* was to be 'a massive armoured charge led by the

The unmistakeable form of a Ju 87G in flight, with the barrels of its 37mm cannon protruding well forward from beneath the wings. This G-2, Wk-Nr 494230 T6+MU, belongs to 10.(Pz)/SG 2 and it was deployed against the Soviet advance into Latvia in mid-1944. (EN Archive)

T-34 across the length and breadth of the Soviet republic of Byelorussia'. Indeed, of more than 2,700 tanks readied for the offensive, the majority were T-34/76s, T-34/85s and SU-85s/100s. Their numbers were around six times greater than the tanks Army Group Centre could muster. Such odds counted, and by January 1945 T-34s of the Red Army's 3rd Byelorussian Front were rolling through East Prussia.

Fighting in East Prussia at this time as *Kommodore* of *Schlachtgeschwader* 2 was Oberst Hans-Ulrich Rudel. By then he had been credited with the destruction of 463 enemy tanks, and was the sole recipient of the Golden Oakleaves with Swords and Diamonds to the Knight's Cross. The *Geschwaderstab* operated both the Ju 87G as well as a few Fw 190s, the former being deployed mainly against enemy armoured breakthroughs which lacked anti-aircraft cover at their spearhead points. Rudel recalled:

A pilot, possibly Oberleutnant Andreas Kuffner, converses with a mechanic beneath the nose of a Ju 87G-2, possibly S7+NU, of 10.(Pz)/SG 3 in 1944 as it undergoes maintenance. Kuffner commanded the *Staffel* from its formation on 7 March 1944 until its redesignation in January 1945. (EN Archive)

A lesser-seen camouflage scheme has been applied to this Ju 87G-1, probably for the winter of 1944–45. The white scribble pattern has been sprayed extensively over the base RLM 70/71 splinter, including over most of the spinner, but not over what appears to be its white tip, nor over the yellow theatre rear fuselage identification band. The underside wingtips also appear to be in yellow, conforming to the requirement for further theatre recognition, while the breech pods on the 37mm cannon have been painted winter white too. (EN Archive)

Stiff fighting in the area around Willkowiscen; the town itself changes hands time and again. A small German armoured unit stands its ground here, supported by us from the first to the last minute of daylight, resisting the incessant onslaught of the Russians for several days. Some of the T-34s take cover behind the corn stooks standing on the harvested fields. We set the stooks on fire with incendiaries so as to uncover the tanks, then we go for them.

A pair of knocked-out T-34s lie either side of the road between Königsberg and Heiligenbeil during the fighting in East Prussia in March 1945. In the foreground is a T-34/85, while behind the trees is a T-34/76 with its turret traversed almost 180 degrees. (Getty Images)

Ju 87G-2 Wk-Nr 494110 is examined by curious GIs at Kitzingen airfield on 8 May 1945 shortly after it was deliberately ground-looped by its pilot, Oberst Hans-Ulrich Rudel, *Kommodore* of SG 2 and the ad hoc *Gefechtsverband Rudel*, prior to him entering captivity. (EN Archive)

By mid-April 1945, just three *Staffeln* – 2.(Pz)/SG 9 (formerly 10.(Pz)/SG 1), 10.(Pz.)/SG 77 under Oberleutnant Maximilian Diepold and 10.(Pz.)/SG 2 under Leutnant Anton Korol – remained operational with the Ju 87G on the Eastern Front, each unit's 12 or so *'Gustavs'* supplemented by some D-5s which were used for bombing and strafing work. With 14 Ju 87s, of which half were serviceable, 10.(Pz.)/SG 77 flew sorties around Bautzen and Cottbus as Red Army and Polish forces thrust towards Dresden. They were joined by 10.(Pz.)/SG 2 later in the month. On 25 April, VIII. *Fliegerkorps* mounted 30 anti-tank sorties.

But ultimately, the 'incessant onslaught' of the Red Army which Rudel describes was too much for Germany's stretched and depleted armies in the East. The T-34, produced in ever greater numbers, went on to spearhead Stalin's tank units all the way to the streets of Berlin, and by May 1945 victory against Nazi Germany had been secured. On the 8th, Oberst Hans-Ulrich Rudel, *Kommodore* of SG 2 and the ad hoc *Gefechtsverband Rudel*, flew into American captivity at Kitzingen airfield in Bavaria, deliberately ground-looping his Ju 87G-2, which tore away the mainwheel legs and smashed the propellers. It was a last act of defiance before surrender.

STATISTICS AND ANALYSIS

On the eve of the invasion of the Soviet Union, the Luftwaffe listed 456 Ju 87s on strength in the East, but by 5 July 1941, less than two weeks later, *Luftflotte* 4 reported just 113 such aircraft available. This reveals a significant drop caused by combat losses, accidents and write-offs in a short period of time. It also demonstrates the level of commitment displayed by the dive-bomber units.

Over the following years, total output of Ju 87s numbered 960 in 1942, 1,672 in 1943 and 1,012 in 1944. The Weser plant at Berlin-Tempelhof had manufactured 960 Ju 87D-3s by mid-1943, while the firm's factory at Bremen-Lemwerder produced 599, equating to a total of 1,559 aircraft. Just 34 Ju 87G-1s were created from D-3 airframes, while 174 G-2s of 208 ordered were finished.

Around 85 per cent of all the Luftwaffe's Ju 87s were based on the Eastern Front by June 1943. Yet, in the wake of Kursk, General Rudolf Meister of the Luftwaffe Operations Staff concluded that because aircraft availability was under strain, and despite the need for anti-tank aircraft in Russia, the Stukas had to be safeguarded as much as possible and, therefore, used against tanks only when they had broken through to rear areas. This never really happened, and the Ju 87 anti-tank *Staffeln* continued to be deployed on a 'fire brigade' basis until the end of the war.

The Soviet Union swamped the Germans with tanks – more than they could deal with. Soviet factories turned out some 100,000 tanks, compared with German output of around 26,000. In addition, Russia received around 12,000 tanks from the Western Allies. However, these figures belie the fact that in the lead-up to *Barbarossa*, many

Having relocated much of its tank production to factories east of the Urals from late 1941, the Soviet Union was able to sustain and increase output without interruption or harassment. Here, freshly produced T-34s in winter white paint wait on railway wagons in the acceptance shop at Zavod No. 183 – the UTZ (Ural Tank Factory) at Nizhny Tagil – in the winter of 1942–43. (Author's Collection)

units in the Red Army suffered from shortages of field workshops, tools, parts and instruction manuals. At the beginning of June 1941, of 892 T-34s delivered to the Red Army, 845 had not been used. Some tank units would not have access to sufficient parts until 1942.

Figures vary slightly for the annual outputs of T-34/76s from the factories at Kharkov, Stalingrad, Nizhniy Tagil, Krasnoye Sormovo, Sverdlovsk, Chelyabinsk and Omsk, but one credible source states that 117 were built in 1940, 3,017 in 1941, 12,527 in 1942, 15,833 in 1943 and 3,976 in 1944 – a total of 35,470 T-34/76s. Soviet figures state that there were 5,400 tanks and assault guns available on 1 January 1944.

The most important centre for T-34 production west of the Urals was Factory No. 112 Krasnoye Sormovo at Gorky, which the Germans believed employed 12,000 workers producing 270 T-34s per month. The massive production effort made by the Soviet factories was required to make good the enormous loss rates borne by T-34-equipped units. In 1943, losses of all types of Soviet tanks stood at 22,400, and in 1944 the figure was 16,900. German losses by comparison averaged – apparently – 6,400 for each year, but then German production was lower.

According to a Soviet source, the Red Army lost 13,800 T-34s in 1944 – 52.7 per cent of the tanks available at the beginning of that year, plus those freshly manufactured during the year. This is an astonishing number. Set against such figures, even the kill rates of pilots such as Rudel, Bromen, Honsberg and Blümel appear insignificant.

AFTERMATH

The T-34 was a war-winning tank – at least by 1945 – thanks to its impressive balance of armour, firepower and speed. The introduction in 1942 of a hexagonal turret allowing more room for movement and, in June 1943, an armoured cupola incorporating five vision blocks for the commander/gunner improved the design further. Yet these upgrades also served to compel improvements in German tank design, although when the T-34/85 appeared in 1944 the Red Army was again able to match the enemy's Panther and Tiger heavy tanks in respect to firepower.

However, according to Klaus Uebe, a Luftwaffe staff officer with considerable experience on the Eastern Front, it was the belief of some German commanders that

A pall of smoke drifts across the sky as a column of troop-laden T-34/85s advances towards the Oder in early 1945. Often the purpose of the troops riding on the back of tanks as 'attached infantry', as seen here, was to counteract enemy anti-tank forces blocking the way. (Getty Images)

the Soviets never grasped the deployment 'art' of massed armour and were content simply to 'grind away' at German air and ground forces.

There is no doubt that the Ju 87's transition from dive-bomber to tank-destroyer at Kursk paid off, and was validated in actions at Belgorod and Orel. But after that, the reality was that the best days of the Ju 87 as a ground-attack aircraft were behind it. With the rapid expansion and accuracy of Soviet anti-aircraft assets, the Stuka became too slow, too cumbersome and too vulnerable. On 10 September 1943, Oberstleutnant Dr. Ernst Kupfer, former *Kommodore* of StG 2 and, from 1 September of that year, the *General der Schlachtflieger*, visited Generalfeldmarschall Erhard Milch at the RLM in Berlin, to whom he presented a blunt report:

> Our losses can all be traced to the fact that the Ju 87s are too slow to come out of their dives and to get out of range, and as a result the enemy anti-aircraft batteries are able to pick them off one after the other. The Ju 87's armour is of little use – a glance at tank armour will help to explain why: even the Tiger and the Panther, with their thick, heavy armour plating, are vulnerable to fire from anti-aircraft and anti-tank guns, as we were able to observe from the air during the operations at Kursk, Belgorod and Orel. Obviously, then, shooting down a heavily-armoured, slow-moving aeroplane at low altitude is no problem at all.
>
> We need an aircraft which is flexible, fast and small enough to be hard to hit, and we need it in sufficient quantity for effective employment. For ground-support operations, then, the single-seater fighter aircraft is the best possible choice.

Lending credence to Kupfer's comments is the fact that one pilot in a Ju 87 anti-tank *Staffel* noted that his unit had lost as many aircraft as the number of tanks it had destroyed. Nevertheless, in 1944, although the Fw 190F and G were intended as the new solution to the problem, there were still 1,012 Ju 87s on strength – an indication of the dire need for ground-attack aircraft. Even then, Ju 87s were assigned to equip the *Nachtschlachtgruppen* (night ground-attack), where it was felt they could operate in a 'safer' environment, and the priority shifted to softer-skinned targets such as troops, transport, supply facilities and airfields.

Berliners watch warily as a column of T-34s rolls into the German capital in May 1945. By this stage, the tank nearest the camera – a T-34/76 built by STZ with a cast hexagonal turret and lacking the commander's cupola – would have been a relatively rare combat 'veteran'. (Thomas Anderson)

After service in World War II, the T-34 continued to be used in post-war conflicts where there was direct or indirect Soviet machination such as in Korea, the Sinai Desert, the Golan Heights, Cuba, North Vietnam, Angola, Yemen and Cyprus. At the time of writing, it is likely that the engineers working on the design and development of the next-generation 'Universal Combat Platform' T-14 Armata at UralVagonZavod at Nizhny Tagil will be mindful of their armour heritage.

FURTHER READING

Armstrong, Richard N., *Red Army Tank Commanders – The Armored Guards* (Schiffer Publishing, Atglen, 1994)

Arthy, Andrew, Dr., *Last Days of the Cannon Bird – Luftwaffe Junkers Ju 87G anti-tank operations on the Eastern Front, April-May 1945* (The Aviation Historian, Issue No. 37, Horsham, 2021)

Askey, Nigel, *The T-34 in WWII: The Legend vs. The Performance* at www.operationbarbarossa.net (accessed 1/8/2021)

Baryatinskiy, Mikhail, *T-34 Medium Tank (1939– 1943)* (Ian Allan Publishing, Hersham, 2007)

Bateson, Richard P., *Stuka! Junkers Ju 87* (Ducimus Books, London, 1972)

Brütting, Georg, *Das waren die deutschen Stuka-Asse, 1939–45* (Motorbuch Verlag, Stuttgart, 1984)

Bryukhov, Vasiliy, *Red Army Tank Commander – At War in a T-34 on the Eastern Front* (Pen & Sword, Barnsley, 2013)

Cooling, Benjamin Franklin, (Ed.), *Air Support* (Office of Air Force History, United States Air Force, Washington D.C., 1990)

Corum, James S. *The Luftwaffe – Creating the Operational Air War, 1918–1940* (University Press of Kansas, Lawrence, 1997)

Corum, James S. and Muller, Richard, *The Luftwaffe's Way of War – German Air Force Doctrine 1911-1945* (The Nautical and Aviation Publishing Company of America, Baltimore, 1998)

Creek, Eddie J., *Junkers Ju 87 – From Dive-Bomber to Tank-Buster 1935–1945* (Classic Publications, Hersham, 2012)

Deichmann, Gen der. Fl. a.D., Paul, *German Air Force Operations in Support of the Army, USAF Historical Studies No. 163* (Arno Press, New York, 1962)

Fleischer, Wolfgang, *German Air-Dropped Weapons to 1945* (Midland Publishing, Hinckley, 2004)

Fleischer, Wolfgang, *T-34 – An Illustrated History of Stalin's Greatest Tank* (Greenhill Books, Barnsley, 2020)

Healy, Mark, *T-34 Tank – 1940 to date (all models)* (Haynes Publishing, Sparkford, 2018)

Hooton, E. R., *Stalin's Claws – From the Purges to the Winter War: Red Army Operations before Barbarossa 1937–1941* (Tattered Flag Press, Pulborough, 2013)

Kay, Antony L, *Junkers Aircraft and Engines 1913–1945* (Putnam Aeronautical Books, London, 2004)

Maiolo, Joe, *Cry Havoc – The Arms Race and the Second World War, 1931–1941* (John Murray London, 2010)

Muller, Richard, *The German Air War in Russia* (The Nautical & Aviation Publishing Co. of America, Baltimore, 1992)

Pulham, Francis, and Kerrs, Will, *T-34 Shock – The Soviet Legend in Pictures* (Fonthill Media, Stroud, 2021)

Samsonov, Peter, *Designing the T-34 – Genesis of the Revolutionary Soviet Tank* (Gallantry Books, Hornscastle, 2019)

Smith, Peter C., *Junkers Ju 87 Stuka* (The Crowood Press, Marlborough, 1998)

Tucker-Jones, Anthony, *Stalin's Armour 1941–1945 – Soviet Tanks at War* (Pen & Sword, Barnsley, 2021)

Uebe, Gen.Lt. a.D., Klaus, *Russian Reactions to German Airpower in World War II, USAF Historical Studies No. 176* (Arno Press, New York, 1964)

Zaloga, Steven J., *Osprey New Vanguard 9 – T-34/76 Medium Tank 1941–45,* (Osprey Publishing, Oxford, 1994)

Zaloga, Steven J., Kinnear, Jim, Aksenov, Andrey and Koshchavtsev, Alexandr, *Soviet Tanks in Combat 1941–1945 – The T-28, T-34, T-34-85 and T-44 Medium Tanks* (Concord Publications Company, Hong Kong, 1997)

INDEX